A Practical Approach to Sixteenth-Century Counterpoint

Robert Gauldin
Eastman School of Music

PRENTICE-HALL, INC.   *Englewood Cliffs, New Jersey 07632*

Library of Congress Cataloging-in-Publication Data

GAULDIN, ROBERT, [date]
    A practical approach to sixteenth-century
counterpoint.

    Bibliography: p. 293
    Includes index.
    1. Counterpoint—16th century.   I. Title.
II. Title: Practical approach to 16th-century
counterpoint.
ML446.G38 1984   781.4'2'09031   84-15989
ISBN 0-13-689258-2

Editorial/production supervision
    and interior design: Lisa A. Domínguez
Page layout: Gail Collis
Cover design: Whitman Studio, Inc.
Manufacturing buyer: Ray Keating

781.42
G 23 p
131713
may 1985

Printed in the United States of America

10 9 8 7 6 5 4 3 2 1

ISBN 0-13-689258-2 01

Prentice-Hall International, Inc., *London*
Prentice-Hall of Australia Pty. Limited, *Sydney*
Editora Prentice-Hall do Brasil, Ltda., *Rio de Janeiro*
Prentice-Hall Canada Inc., *Toronto*
Prentice-Hall of India Private Limited, *New Delhi*
Prentice-Hall of Japan, Inc., *Tokyo*
Prentice-Hall of Southeast Asia Pte. Ltd., *Singapore*
Whitehall Books Limited, *Wellington, New Zealand*

Contents

4

MELODIC WRITING WITH BLACK NOTES   36

Text Setting with Black Notes   39

5

TWO-VOICE TEXTURE WITH BLACK NOTES   42

6

OTHER ASPECTS OF TWO-VOICE TEXTURE   48

Double Counterpoint   48
Canonic Writing in Two Voices   53
Aspects of Structure in Vocal Two-Voice Compositions   55
Instrumental Writing in Two-Voice Texture   60

7

EXAMPLES OF TWO-VOICE COMPOSITIONS FOR ANALYSIS   63

8

THREE-VOICE TEXTURE WITH WHITE NOTES   76

Harmonic Resources   76
Voice-Leading Between Consonant Sonorities   79
Dissonance with White Notes   82

9

CADENCES IN THREE-VOICE TEXTURE;
OTHER WHITE-NOTE DISSONANCE   87

Cadences in Three Voices   87
Other White-Note Dissonance   92

10

BLACK NOTES IN THREE-VOICE TEXTURE;
IMITATION AND REENTRIES   96

Imitation and Reentry in Three-Voice Texture   98

Preface

The purpose of this text is twofold: the acquisition of writing skills in the contrapuntal discipline, and the simulation of sixteenth-century sacred polyphonic idioms. As such, its manner of presentation is basically practical in nature. It does not propose any single comprehensive analytical system other than a consideration of those compositional techniques contained in the music, nor does it focus on such matters as historical evolution or comparisons of various schools or individual composers, except for occasional commentary. Historical terminology, drawn from treatises of the period, will be inserted where appropriate.[1]

The material in this text is intended for use by upper undergraduate or graduate students. Although no previus contrapuntal training is necessary, some acquaintance with Baroque polyphonic terminology may prove helpful. The didactic method utilized is that of a "non-species" or "direct" approach. In this respect it follows the groundwork laid down by Soderlund, Morris, and others.[2] A discussion of the species system as advocated by Fux is included in appendix 1.[3] While the use of species to introduce contrapuntal concepts is a valuable discipline, particularly as a prerequisite to layer or linear analysis in tonal music,[4] its employment does necessitate a considerable amount of time in presentation. As a result, many modal counterpoint texts emphasize only two- and three-voice writ-

---

[1]Standard Latin as well as Italian terms drawn from contemporary theorists (such as Zarlino) are included.

[2]See the list of counterpoint texts in the annotated bibliography.

[3]In addition to Fux, earlier treatises which anticipate his species technique are quoted.

[4]See for instance, Felix Salzer and Carl Schachter, *Counterpoint in Composition* (New York: McGraw-Hill Book Company, 1969).

ing, when, in reality, the textural norm of the period is more often four or five parts. In addition, the student may never come to grips with certain polyphonic techniques typical of the sixteenth century; namely, paraphrase and parody procedures, the use of a cantus firmus in a tenor mass, familiar style, triple meter, polychoral writing, and chromaticism. This text has attempted to "push forward" through the earlier material in order that these topics may be presented more fully, and appropriate exercises assigned.

Unless otherwise indicated, the musical examples illustrating specific devices have been composed by the author. In order to demonstrate the possibility of employing a single given pitch series within the contexts of different compositional techniques, a five-note motive has been arbitrarily chosen to serve as a unifying thread throughout the text. In addition to the examples included within the chapters, a collection of complete movements or excerpts drawn from music literature is included at the conclusion of each major textural division for study by the student; for instance, see chapter 12, which contains six three-voice works. Although no particular analytical "system" is advocated, the brief comments preceding each piece serve to draw attention to certain interesting features of the composition. Most of these are in the sacred vocal idiom, although a few secular and instrumental selections are included. The composers represented span the sixteenth-century repertory, with emphasis given to Palestrina and the Counter-Reformation sacred style. A few figures, such as Josquin or Morley have been added to illustrate older as well as more progressive tendencies. The date of composition or publication is given for the various examples when known.

Writing assignments are suggested at appropriate points in the text. Their number is somewhat minimal, as it is assumed that the instructor will doubtless wish to supplement these with projects of his or her own, depending upon the progress of the students and the specific difficulties they may be encountering. The setting up of isolated devices, such as suspensions, can often be worked out in class at the blackboard. Bear in mind, however, that excessive time spent in perfecting the material of the earlier chapters may necessitate the omission of many of the later topics. It is the author's experience that each new device does not have to be mastered completely before moving on to the next. After all, these same problems and situations will continue to arise in subsequent assignments, and thus allow additional opportunities for correction.

The three appendices deal with Species Counterpoint, the Mass, and the historical placement of various composers in this period. A selected annotated bibliography of texts, treatises, anthologies, and a list of related books, articles, and analyses are included, along with an index of terms and musical selections.

The author wishes to acknowledge his debt to the long-suffering students in his course on Renaissance counterpoint, which served as the testing ground for the assignments in this text.

1

Preliminary
Remarks

THE FORMAT OF THE MUSIC

The sacred choir of the Late Renaissance consisted exclusively of male
voices. The men took the *bassus* and *tenor* parts, while young boys, whose
voices had not yet changed, were assigned to the *altus* and *cantus* or
superius (soprano). Any additional parts required beyond this four-voice
format were simply indicated by a numerical designation (*quintus, sextus,*
etc.). A *quintus* part, for instance, might correspond to a second tenor or
soprano in modern terms.

A variety of clefs are employed in the manuscripts of the time. These
include the C clefs (soprano, mezzo-soprano, alto, and tenor), the G clef
(treble), and the F clefs (for bass and occasionally baritone). The five-line
staff is standard by this time. The use of the various clefs is based largely
on the avoidance of excessive ledger lines. The format for choir may best be
thought of in terms of a ten-line system. There are two methods of
distributing the clefs, dependent on range considerations. The use of the
higher clefs comprises the so-called *chiavette* system, employing the treble,
mezzo-soprano, alto, and tenor *or* baritone clefs (see Figs. 1-1A). The *chiavi
naturali* system is basically a third lower, using the soprano, alto, tenor,
and bass clefs (Fig. 1-1B).

Fig. 1-2 converts these two systems to modern clef usage, illustrating
the vocal range of each voice without resorting to the use of ledger lines.

FIGURE 1-1   The two basic clef systems in the 16th century

FIGURE 1-2   Voice ranges according to clef system

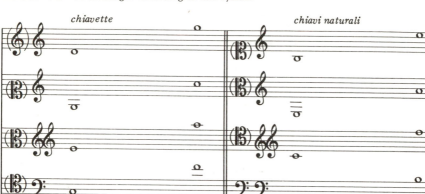

This text will employ only the familiar treble and bass clefs, with the tenor voice using a double treble clef, (𝄞𝄞) sounding an octave lower.

The great bulk of this music exists in the form of individual voice parts, since very few "full scores" have survived to the present day. Many composers doubtless employed a working score to facilitate the calculation of the various polyphonic lines in a piece. However, once the specific voice parts were copied, the score was apparently discarded.[1]

The voice parts exist in two formats, *choir books* and *part books.* In the former the separate parts are written on two facing pages of a folio (for example, see Fig. 1-3). The performers stood around a lectern and read from the same pages. With part books, the separate voice parts for a number of different compositions were copied in a single volume (such as an *altus* book). One or more singers of that voice would then read the part together. This procedure was probably more common with larger ensembles, although it must be stressed that most of the choirs at that time were fairly small by modern standards. A typical page from a *cantus* and *altus* instrumental part book is reproduced in Ex. 6-15. In either case, the singer had only his particular vocal line and could not follow the progress of the other voices from a full score. There is iconographic evidence that one of the

---

[1]For some examples of extant full scores see Edward E. Lowinsky, "Early Scores in Manuscript," *Journal of the American Musicological Society,* 13 (1960), 126–73.

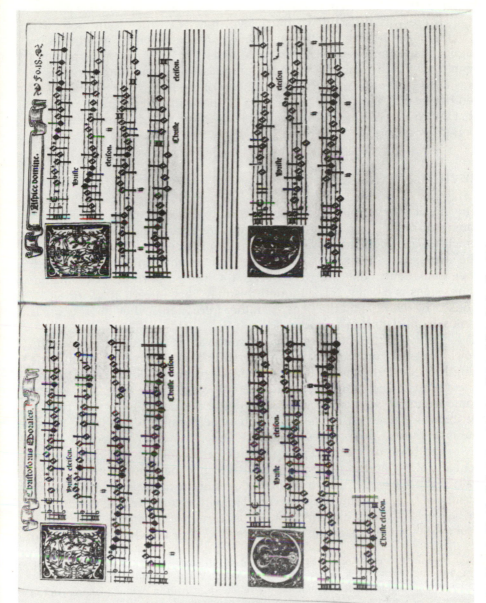

FIGURE 1-3 Choirbook format — Morales: Christe (*Missa Aspice Domine*)

singers may have acted as a kind of conductor, even to the extent of using a baton.[2] Little is known of possible rehearsal techniques during this period.

There was no standard pitch level that was universally accepted. Some scholars believe that the music may have been about one whole step higher than our present standard of a' = 440Hz.[3] The singers apparently employed a rather thin nasal sound, emphasizing a pure tone; no vibrato was used. Although the sacred polyphony of the Late Renaissance has often been called the "Golden Age" of á cappella singing, there is evidence that the church choirs were often doubled with instruments or at least supported by an organ.[4]

RHYTHM

The music of the Late Renaissance commonly employs note values of longer duration than those to which we are accustomed in present-day practice. The frequency of values of a half-note or greater has given rise to the expression "white notation." The various rhythmic durations with their Latin equivalents are given in Fig. 1-4. The proportion between adjacent values is usually 2:1, although this may vary in certain metric situations.[5] The *maxima* and the *longa* are rather infrequent, while the *semifusa* is almost nonexistent in vocal music.

The use of ties between adjacent note values does not appear in the voice parts of this period.[6] Therefore, the basic means of altering the length of the durations in Fig. 1-4 is through the employment of the *dot* (*punctus additionis*), which adds one-half the value to the note. As a result, some rhythmic durations (such as ♩ ♪) are not possible, as they cannot be expressed without the tie. Those rules pertaining to the metric placement of various note values will be discussed later in chapter 2.

The basic unit of rhythmic measure, analogous to our present-day whole note, was the *tactus* or *battuta*, which equaled one breve (|o|) in value. The subsequent rhythmic breakdown of the *tactus* is normally by divisions of two, resulting in the so-called imperfect time (*Tempus imperfectum* or |o| = o o), and imperfect prolation (*Prolatio imperfecta* or o = ♩♩). The resultant meter signature is expressed as ₵ or C, which is equivalent

[2]See the two plates on p. 193 of Walter Salem, *Musikleben im 16. Jahrhundert*, Band III, Lfg. 8 of *Musikgeschichte im Bildern* (Leipzig: Deutscher Verlag für Musik, 1976).

[3]The difficulties of ascertaining pitch level are dealt with in Arthur Mendel, *Pitch in Western Music since 1500: A Re-examination* (Basel: Bärenreiter Kassel, 1979).

[4]See Howard Mayer Brown, "Performing Practice; 15th and 16th Century Music," *The New Grove Dictionary of Music and Musicians*, Vol. 14, (London: Macmillan Pub. Ltd., 1980), pp. 377–383.

[5]For further information see the section on triple meter in chapter 16.

[6]Some of the manuscripts in Lowinsky's "Early Scores" show the use of both ties and bar lines; see plates 10 and 15.

FIGURE 1-4 Note durations used in the 16th century

▭	Maxima			
▭	Longa			
▭	Breve	=	Double whole note	▯
◊	Semibreve	=	Whole note	o
↓	Minim	=	Half note	𝅗𝅥
↓	Semiminim	=	Quarter note	♩
♪	Fusa	=	Eighth note	♪
♪	Semifusa	=	Sixteenth note	♬

to our 2/1 meter.[7] Each *tactus* or measure contains two "pulse-beats" or semibreves. The twofold division of the semibreve in turn produces a "simple" background of two minims. The tempo or rate of speed for the semibreve is thought to lie between M.M. 48 and M.M. 64.

For pedagogical purposes the meter signature ₵ may be thought of as 4/2, with each minim (or half-note) receiving one "beat" of approximately M.M. 96. By thus dividing each *tactus* or measure into four distinct beats, it will be easier to relate the handling of consonance and dissonance to specific metric positions. These will be referred to hereafter as "beats 1, 2, 3, or 4." All of the musical examples in the first section of this text will employ duple (or imperfect) time exclusively. For a discussion of triple meter and proportional relationships, see chapter 16.

The individual voice parts are normally written without bar lines. The few one does encounter apparently denote phrasing or formal divisions within the music. Ex. 1-1 contains three versions of the same melodic passage. In Ex. 1-1A the original notation appears with no bar lines. This passage is transcribed into modern notational practice in Ex. 1-1B; note that the use of bar lines necessitates the incorporation of ties for those notes extending over the bar. This text will employ a compromise procedure (called *Mensurstriche*), in which the division by bars is denoted with a short vertical stroke extending only halfway down through the staff. Ties will be omitted, thus retaining the original durations (see Ex. 1-1C). In the case of polyphonic music the bar lines will be drawn between the staves.

---

[7]For a further distinction between C and ₵ see *prolation canon* in chapter 6.

EXAMPLE 1-1

Gombert: *O gloriosa Dei genitrix* (motet)

THE ECCLESIASTICAL MODES

The tonal organization of the sacred music in the sixteenth century finds its roots in the modal system of *plainsong* or *Gregorian chant*. Although the modality of the Late Renaissance is vastly different from this early type of monody, it is wise to review a few basic premises of medieval modal practice. Since many polyphonic works of the sixteenth century are based on specific Gregorian tunes, their tonal structure is in turn influenced by the mode of the particular chant employed.

The adage that practice precedes theory is appropriate in this case. The modal terminology of the Greeks[8] was resurrected by medieval theorists to systematize the already preexistent literature of chant. Plainsong used as its fundamental tonal material the seven "white-note" pitch classes (A B C D E F G plus B♭). B natural was denoted with a square-shaped b (♮ or *quadratum*) whereas B flat used a rounded b (♭ or *rotundum*). There are three basic characteristics which determined the particular mode of a chant melody.

Of paramount importance is the last note of the chant, the so-called *finalis* of the mode. This concluding tone is customarily on either D, E, F, or G, denoting the Dorian, Phrygian, Lydian, and Mixolydian modes respectively.[9] There are occasional exceptions to this principle. [10]

The modes are classified according to the approximate range within which the melody fell. Each mode has two distinct *species*: (1) the *authentic* form, from *finalis* to *finalis* (or in the case of Dorian from d to d') and (2) the

---

[8]For a summary of Greek modal practice see R. P. Winnington-Ingram, "Greece 7-9," *The New Grove Dictionary of Music and Musicians*. Vol. 7, pp. 664–68.

[9]The names of the modes refer to Grecian tribes and geographical areas and as such should always be capitalized.

[10]For instance, a Lydian tune might sometimes cadence on a final A rather than an F.

plagal form, a perfect fourth lower than authentic (or in the case of Dorian from A to a). The *plagal* forms are indicated by the prefix Hypo; thus Dorian = d to d' and Hypodorian = A to a. A numbering system of the resultant octave species is often employed (see Fig. 1-5).[11] Bear in mind that this classification by approximate octave span is often very arbitrary, as some chants do not fall easily into either the authentic or plagal mode.

One particular tone of each mode (other than the *finalis*) is employed for reciting lengthy syllabic texts, as in the case of the Psalms. This *reciting* or *psalm tone* (also called the *tenor* of the mode) is usually a perfect fifth above the *finalis* in the authentic modes. It also functions as an important cadential pitch within the mode.[12]

Examine Fig. 1-5, which summarizes the basic points of the previous discussion.

FIGURE 1-5   Modal octave species in Gregorian chant

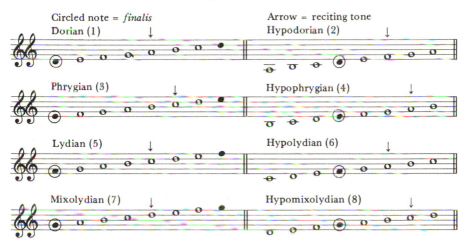

The chant melody in Ex. 1-2 appears in both its original chant notation[13] and in modern transcription. It is in the seventh mode; note the frequent use of the reciting tone d'.

[11]In addition to the numbering of the eight modes, they are also referred to as *Protus* (Dorian), *Deuterus* (Phrygian), *Tritus* (Lydian), and *Tetrardus* (Mixolydian). In the sixteenth century composers often used the term *tonus* preceded by the numerical designation (Primus tonus = Dorian authentic, Quartus tonus = Hypophrygian, etc.).

[12]Several important studies of Gregorian chant have appeared recently that attempt to reveal its underlying tonal organization and possible origins. See Finn Egeland Hansen, *The Grammar of Gregorian Chant* (Copenhagen: Dan Fog Musikforlag, 1976) and Hendrik van der Werf, *The Emergence of Gregorian Chant* (Rochester, NY: Hendrik van der Werf, 1983).

[13]For a summary of plainsong notation see the preface to *Liber Usualis*, ed. Benedictines of Solesmes (Tournai: Desclée et cie, 1961).

EXAMPLE 1-2

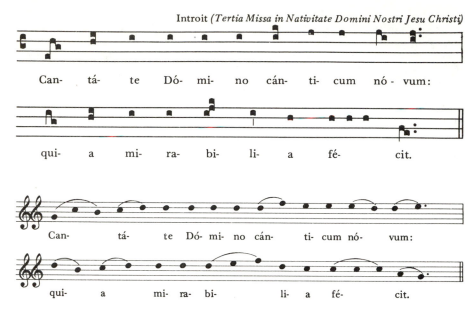

Introit *(Tertia Missa in Nativitate Domini Nostri Jesu Christi)*

Can- tá- te Dó- mi- no cán- ti- cum nó - vum:

qui- a mi- ra- bi- li- a fé- cit.

Can- tá- te Dó- mi- no cán- ti- cum nó- vum:

qui- a mi- ra- bi- li- a fé- cit.

Some texts have borrowed the terms "tonic" and "dominant" from common practice in tonal theory to replace the *finalis* and reciting tones respectively. However, this procedure is questionable. Although there are instances of chant tunes in which those tones do give one an aural impression similar in effect to tonic and dominant, this concept of functionality is not consistent with sixteenth-century theory and should be discouraged. Sing the plainsong melody in Ex. 1-3; the *finalis* and reciting tones are E and A respectively. Do they resemble the usual "tonic-dominant" relationships?

EXAMPLE 1-3

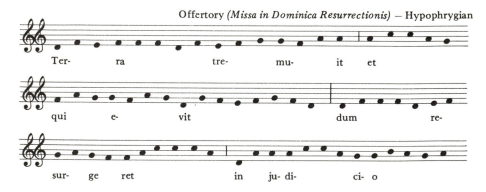

Offertory *(Missa in Dominica Resurrectionis)* — Hypophrygian

Ter- ra tre- mu- it et

qui e- vit dum re-

sur- ge ret in ju- di- ci- o

De-   us   Al-

le-

lu- ja.

As noted previously, B♭ is the only accidental encountered in chant. It was used to avoid a direct melodic tritone B and F (the so-called *diabolus in musica*, (see Ex. 1-4A), to correct an implied tritone in the melodic contour (Ex. 1-4B), or to "soften" the upper neighbor to the pitch class A (A B♭ A), as shown in Ex. 1-4C. In fact, this relation of B♭ to F and A, which are both important structural tones in the Lydian and Dorian modes, may have eventually changed the basic characteristics of those modes. Thus Lydian with consistent B♭s became the Ionian mode (our present major), while Dorian with consistent B♭s became the Aeolian mode (our present natural minor). However, the Ionian and Aeolian systems were not officially recognized until the sixteenth century.[14]

EXAMPLE 1-4

A.   B.   C.

In order to facilitate the memorization of chants which were largely *melismatic* (that is, one text syllable to many notes), a *solmization* method was instituted. This *hexachordal* system assigns particular syllables to the various pitch classes. Thus, in the *naturale* hexachord C = Ut, D = Re, E = Mi, F = Fa, G = Sol, and A = La.[15] As the melody moves into a range that falls outside this major sixth, a *mutation* process occurs, in which the original syllables are reassigned to hexachords on G (*durum* or hard, because of the presence of B♮) and F (*molle* or soft, because of the presence of B♭) . Care is taken so the half-step always falls on Mi-Fa (E-F in *naturale*, B-C in

[14]Glareanus' *Dodecachordon* (1547) as the title implies, declared the existence of twelve modes, including the authentic and plagal forms of the Ionian and Aeolian.

[15]These syllables supposedly originated from the first word of each successive phrase of the hymn *Ut queant laxis* (Ut, Resonare, Mira, Famuli, Solve,Labii).

FIGURE 1-6   The hexachord system

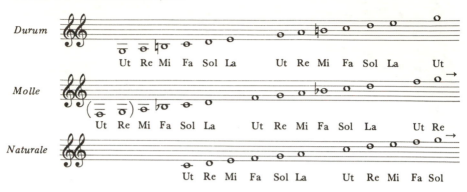

durum, and A-B♭ in *molle*). Thus, the sequence of tone-tone-semitone-tone-tone is maintained in each hexachord. This system is illustrated in Fig. 1-6.

A short phrase utilizing this approach is given in Ex. 1-5. Note the mutational process.

EXAMPLE 1-5

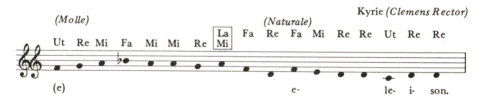

By the Late Renaissance, centuries of polyphonic practice had drastically altered many of the modal principles noted in plainsong. The Ionian and Aeolian modes, with *finalis* on C and A respectively, are added. Any example of Lydian usually contains a high percentage of B♭s. This accidental is also encountered in the other modes, particularly Dorian. In addition to the B♭, certain raising accidentals may be noted in the polyphony of the period: C♯, F♯, and G♯. The fact that they are not always written in the music by the composer but were probably meant to be added by the performer, accounts for the term *musica ficta* (or false music). All sharp and natural signs are denoted by a single symbol ♯, which resembles our present-day sharp. The degree to which *musica ficta* is applied to the music remains a point of argument among many scholars today. For that reason, unless they are specifically notated in the original sources, they will hereafter in this text be indicated by a sharp *above* the designated note. These raising accidentals are employed for several different purposes. Their main use is in cadential formulas, either final or interior, to supply a half-step or "leading tone" below the cadence tone. (see Ex. 1-6A). Obviously, the Lydian (E-F) and Ionian (B-C) modes already contain the necessary half-step. The Phrygian mode continues to use its inverted leading-tone F-E, without altering the D or F of the cadential formula. These sharps are also employed to retain specific intervallic relationships between imitating voices. In this respect they are usually supplied by the composer (see Ex. 1-6B). Note that F♯ is never used to "correct" the tritone B and F. Finally, they sometimes appear as "color tones" in contrast to the basic white-note diatonic harmonies, although this procedure occurs more commonly in homorhythmic settings (see Ex. 1-6C and chapter 13).

EXAMPLE 1-6

It was possible to transpose the entire modal system up a perfect fourth, resulting in a key signature of one flat. Thus, Dorian was now on G, Lydian on B♭, etc. This in turn also affects the available accidentals: B♭ = E♭, C♯ = F♯, F♯ = B♮, and G♯ = C♯.

The modal classification of chant was intended to serve a basically monodic music. With the advent of polyphonic practice, however, theorists were divided as to whether to consider the modal characteristics of each separate voice, or the use of an overall modal designation for the entire piece. By the Late Renaissance the determination of the mode of a composition was complicated by a number of factors. In order to understand the principles at work in this music, it is necessary to review briefly the historical evolution of polyphonic composition from its inception to the middle of the sixteenth century. The earliest attempts (around 900) consisted of setting a counterpoint against a given chant melody in the *tenor*. The *tenor*, therefore, maintained the modal characteristic of the plainsong. In the freer polyphony of later periods, the *tenor* dropped its association with a given chant, although it still continued to function as the foundational voice above which the other parts were composed. From the fifteenth through the early sixteenth centuries, the *cantus* and *tenor* emerged as a structural duet, displaying the basic modal properties of the piece, while the *altus* and *bassus* remained somewhat modally neutral.[16] Thus, the mode of a composition could usually be determined by examining the *finalis* of the *tenor*. Indeed, one of the contemporary theorists of the period, Pietro Aron, states emphatically that the singer should determine the mode of a composition from the *tenor* voice.[17] From about the middle of the sixteenth century, however, the addition of the Ionian and Aeolian modes and the dependence upon the *bassus* as the harmonic foundation tended to undermine the older concepts. As Reese points out, in most situations the *finalis* of the mode is contained in both the *tenor* and *bassus* voices.[18] It may be noted that in the Phrygian mode the *bassus* is more likely to cadence on the *finalis* in pieces of more than three voices. Undue emphasis should not be placed necessarily on the last note as a mode-determining tone, since Zarlino warns that " . . . although some would have us judge a composition by its final . . . It does not follow from this that we may come to recognize the mode on which a composition is based by this alone."[19] Perhaps of equal importance are the opening pitch classes of a piece and the tones chosen for cadential punctuation in the interior of the work. Fig. 1-7 summarizes this information, illustrating the most common *finalis*, initial notes, and cadence points that are most typical of each authentic mode.[20]

The question of modality in polyphonic music will be explored further during the discussion of two- and three-voice texture.

LATIN PRONUNCIATION

Greek was the prevailing language of the earliest Christians. Not only were the New Testament scriptures written in Greek, but evidence of Hellenistic philosophical and literary influence may be noted, as in portions of John's

---

[16]Bernhard Meier, *Die Tonarten der Klassischen Vokalpolyphonie* (Utrecht: Oosthoek, Scheltema, and Holkema, 1974) explores the question of polyphonic modality in great depth. Although this work is not available in English, a translation is being prepared by Ellen Beebe. An example summary on current thought in this area may be found in David Stern, "Tonal Organization in Modal Polyphony," *Theory and Practice* 6/2 (1981), pp. 5-11.

[17]Pietro Aron, *Trattato della natura et cognitione di tutti gli tuoni di canto figurato* (1525).

[18]Gustave Reese, *Music in the Renaissance* (New York: W. W. Norton & Company, Inc., 1954), p. 182.

[19]This quotation from Zarlino's *Le Institutioni harmoniche* is cited in Oliver Strunk, *Source Readings in Music History* (New York: W. W. Norton & Company, Inc., 1950), p. 134.

[20]Based on the research in Knud Jeppesen, *Counterpoint: The Polyphonic Vocal Style of the Sixteenth Century*, tr. by Glen Hayden (Englewood Cliffs, NJ: Prentice-Hall, Inc., 1939), pp. 81–82 and Gustave Soderlund, *Direct Approach to Counterpoint in Sixteenth-Century Style* (Englewood Cliffs, NJ: Prentice-Hall, Inc., 1947), pp. 15–17.

FIGURE 1-7 Mode-defining tones in the 16th century

Mode	Finalis	First Tones	Most Frequent Interior Cadences	Less Frequent Interior Cadences
Dorian	D	A, D	D, A, F	G
Phrygian	E	E, A, (B)	E, A, G	C
Lydian	F	F, C	F, C, A	D
Mixolydian	G	G, D	G, D, C	A
Aeolian	A	A, E, (D)	A, D, C	G
Ionian	C	C, G	C, G, A	D

Gospel. However, by the end of the second century, such Church fathers as Irenaeus and Ignatius recognized the seat of authority as resting in the church at Rome and its bishop. As this position was subsequently strengthened in the following centuries, Latin gradually replaced Greek as the official language of Christendom.[21] Jerome's translation of the Bible into Latin, the so-called *Vulgate* (about 405 A.D.), marked an end to the ancient Roman language and led to the eventual establishment of medieval Latin.

Ecclesiastical Latin, as used in the liturgy of the Roman Church, differs in minor respects from the classical language of the Caesars. In addition to a slight change in the alphabet (both U and V are used), the pronunciation of certain vowel-consonant combinations is modified and softened. The result is strikingly similar to modern Italian in some instances. A rather complete pronunciation guide is provided below for the purpose of singing with Latin texts.

1. Single Vowels
    A = short a (ă) as in car (ad = ăd, facta = fă - ctă)
    E = either short e (ĕ) as in bet (et = ĕt, amen = a - mĕn) or long e (ā) as in prey (te = tā, Patre = Pa - trā)
    I = long i (ē) as in marine (vitam = vē - tam, finis = fē - nēs)
    O= long o (ō) as in old (Deo = De - ō, nobis = nō - bis)
    O= short o (ŏ) as in nought (Dominum = Dŏ - mi - um)
    U= long u (ū) as in rule (tu = tū, solus = so - lūs)
    Y= same as I above
2. Multiple Vowels
    With two or more consecutive vowels, each is pronounced *separately* (De - um, con - fi - te - or, Fil - i - us, etc.)
    The basic exceptions are:
    a. AE and OE, which are pronounced with a long Latin e (ā), as in bonae (bo - nā) and coelum (chā - lum)
    b. QU followed by another vowel, as in qui (kwē, not qu - i) and quō (kwō)

[21]An occasional Greek phrase or sentence may be noted in Latin liturgy, as in the case of the Kyrie of the Ordinary of the Mass.

3. Single Consonants

    C =   hard k as in cold (credo = kre - do); but before E,I,Y,AE, and OE it
          sounds CH as in cello (pacem = pa - chem)

    G =   hard g as in cigar (gloria = glo - ri- a); but before E,I,Y,AE, and OE it
          sounds j as in gem (genitum = je - ni - tum)

    H =   is silent (except in mihi and nihil, where it sounds a hard k = mi - ki
          and ni -kil)

    J =   y as in year (alleluja = al - le - lu - ya)

    S =   s as in sin (solus = so - lus)

    All others pronounced as in English

4. Multiple Consonants

    CC = k as in accord (ecclesium = e - kle - si - um); but *followed* by E,I,Y,AE,
          and OE it sounds ch as in Bocce (acceperant = a - che - pe - rant)

    CH = k as in chaos (Christe = Kris - te)

    GN = ny as in canyon (agnes = an - yus)

    SC followed by E,I,Y,AE, and OE = sh as in sheperd (descendit =
        de-shen-dit)

    TH = hard t as in Thomas (catholicam = ca - to - li - cam)

    TI followed by a vowel and preceded by any letter except S,T, or X =
        tséé (gratias = gra - stee - as, tertia = ter - tsee - a)

    XC before E or I = KSH (excelsis = ek - shel - sis)

    Double consonants are usually pronounced separately (tol-lis, Ho-san-na)

The stressed syllable of a word is generally the first or second syllable.
Since accentuation is so crucial to the rhythmic setting of words to music,
the Latin texts of musical selections included in this work will be scanned
for strong and weak syllables. All translations furnished will strive to be as
literal as possible, even to the occasional detriment of the meaning of the
sentence:

Plé-ni	sunt	cáe-	li	et	tér-	ra	gló-	ri-	a	tú-	a.
Full	are	heaven	and	earth		glory			of your.	

(Heaven and earth are full of your glory).

In many instances in polyphonic movements, reentries of thematic
material are not underlaid with appropriate text in the original part books.
These texts usually have been supplied by editors of modern editions, as
will be the case in this work with examples of this nature taken from the
literature.

2

Melodic Writing with White Notes

Before taking up the problem of two-voice polyphony, it is essential that those characteristics of the individual melodic line in Late Renaissance sacred music be established. In order to keep the available rhythmic resources to a minimum for the present, only white-note durations will be employed in this chapter. The question of black-note melodic idioms will be discussed in chapter 4.

Verbal descriptions of a particular melodic style are often problematic. Adjectives such as "noble" or "unified" may apply to the linear characteristics of a variety of historical periods. Nevertheless, some general remarks are in order. An aesthetic principle of the Counter-Reformation sacred style is that the music should be serene, objective, and beautifully proportioned. Jeppesen's remarks are appropriate in this regard:

> The linear treatment of the Palestrina music reveals a marked inner coherence and an understanding of what is, in the truest sense, organic, which is indeed sought after in every style species. It abhors the rough and inelegant and rejoices in the free and natural. It avoids strong, unduly sharp accents and extreme contrasts of every kind and expresses itself always in a characteristically smooth and pleasing manner that may seem at first somewhat uniform and unimposing but that soon reveals a richly shaded expression of a superior culture. . . . An absolute, completely free balance between the elements is required; no one element could be emphasized at the expense of another; everything must work together smoothly and harmoniously.[1]

---

[1]Jeppesen, *Counterpoint,* p. 83.

In composing melodic lines in this style, the student must remember above all that this is essentially *vocal* music. Probably the best test for an original melody is for one to sing it. If difficulties or problems arise during performance, there is usually something technically wrong. The opening thematic statements from a number of sections in Palestrina's *Missa brevis* are quoted in Ex. 2-1. Although they contain black notes, which will be discussed in detail in chapter 4, the student is urged to sing and study them carefully in regard to the following sections dealing with pitch succession, overall melodic contour, rhythmic handling, and text setting.

EXAMPLE 2-1

Palestrina: *Missa brevis*

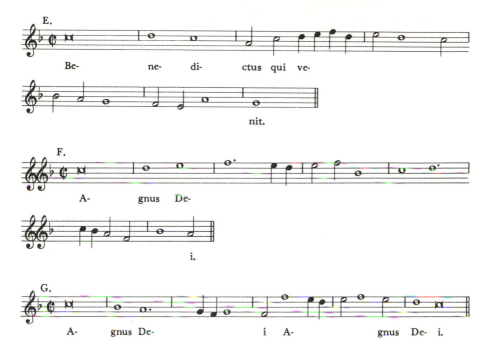

PITCH SUCCESSION
IN THE MELODIC LINE

Some generalities regarding the pitch elements in melodic lines (*melodia*) may be observed. As concerns consecutive melodic intervals, diatonic seconds, thirds, perfect fourths, perfect fifths, and octaves are common. Sixths are found in ascending motion only, and here the minor sixth is preferred.[2] All sevenths, as well as any diminished or augmented intervals, are to be avoided. This rule automatically outlaws the tritone (augmented fourth or diminished fifth) or any chromatic line that employs an augmented prime (such as C-C♯). One may occasionally observe a rest interrupting a leap of a sixth or a seventh, producing a so-called "dead interval"; this is usually encountered after an interior cadence. Although leaps may occur to any pitch class, the note B♮ is handled with care. Ascending leaps to this tone are rare.

As regards melodic motion and contour, this style features basically stepwise movement. In general, the larger the melodic interval, the less it tends to occur. Some observations regarding melodic leaps follow.

[2] Aside from the fact that intervals of sixths are somewhat difficult to sing accurately, many sixths (such as D up to B, or F down to A) require continual mutational changes in the hexachordal solmization.

After ascending or descending stepwise motion, it is unusual to find leaps larger than a third that continue in the *same* direction. Leaps generally occur at the top or bottom of a line when moving in the same direction, not in the middle (Ex. 2-2A). After a leap, the melodic motion usually changes by step or leap in the opposite direction. The larger the leap, the greater the need for this restoring movement. This continual balancing of the line in some ways adheres to a hypothesis of Leonard Meyer, which suggests that the spacial gap created by a melodic leap tends to be filled in eventually with stepwise motion.[3] In this regard consult Ex. 2-2B.

EXAMPLE 2-2

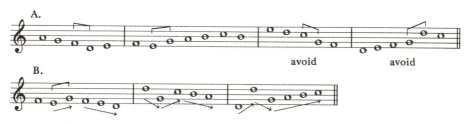

Certain leaps in succession, however, are permitted. These include the outlining of major or minor triads, usually in root position or second inversion (Ex. 2-3A), the partitioning of the octave with successive leaps of fourths and fifths (Ex. 2-3B), as well as the occasional double leap D-A-C in ascending motion, sometimes noted in the Dorian mode (Ex. 2-3C). Following any double leap, the line will almost always change direction.

EXAMPLE 2-3

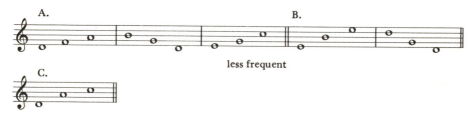

More than two repeated notes are to be avoided for the present, as they are not particularly characteristic of polyphonic texture (Ex. 2-4A).[4] Care will be exercised in melodic sequences of more than one reiteration (Ex. 2-4B), although a single sequence of fourths may be found (Ex. 2-4C).

---

[3]For a discussion of this principle see Leonard B. Meyer, *Explaining Music: Essays and Explorations* (Berkeley: University of California Press, 1973), pp. 145–57.

Also, consult David Lewin, "An Interesting Global Rule for Species Counterpoint," *In Theory Only* 6/8 (1983), pp. 19–44, where a similar concept is applied to first species counterpoint.

[4]Repeated notes will be discussed under the heading Familiar Style in chapter 13.

EXAMPLE 2-4

B♭ may be found as an accidental in all modes; however, its use is more common in Dorian or Lydian, where the F is an important structural note. The interval of a tritone must always be corrected with a B♭ (or an E♭ in the transposed modes), *never* with an F♯. In addition, short melodic passages whose upper and lower limits outline an augmented fourth are to be avoided. Instances involving the diminished fifth are not as crucial in this respect. As mentioned earlier, pertaining to hexachordal theory, the B♭ is often found as an upper neighbor of A (A - B♭ - A) or Mi-Fa-Mi. For the use of B♭ in melodic lines consult the illustrations in Ex. 2-5.

EXAMPLE 2-5

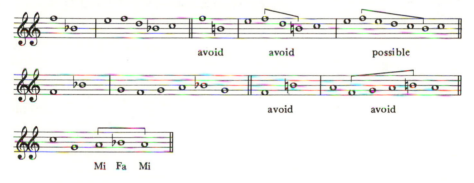

For the time being, the use of all raising accidentals will be restricted to cadences. The final cadence-tone is always approached from above or below by stepwise motion. For those cadences on D, G, and A the penultimate lower tone is raised by a C♯, F♯, or G♯ respectively.[5] Cadences on E, F, or C do not require *musica ficta*. In the transposed modes these will appear a perfect fourth higher, of course. Study the various melodic cadences in Ex. 2-6. For appropriate beginning and interior cadence tones, consult Fig. 1-7 as regards the various modal preferences.

Some general guidelines for overall melodic contour may be noted. The highest (peak) and lowest (valley) notes of a melody are crucial tonal events, and it is essential that their role not be diminished by undue repetition (Ex. 2-7A). Continual reiteration or periodic return to a single pitch in the melodic line, thereby creating a prevailing static motion with little sense of directed motion (Ex. 2-7B), is, likewise, to be avoided. This per-

---

[5]A Phrygian approach to A via G and B♭ is also possible.

EXAMPLE 2-6

tains, as well, to a melody in which the pitches of a particular triad are constantly stressed; one must strive to distribute the tonal interest in such a way that most of the available diatonic notes receive some attention (Ex. 2-7C). Although simple scalar passages, often even encompassing the range of an octave, may be found, this basic stepwise motion is commonly disguised through momentary "diversions" in the line. Thus an overall step-progression emerges, securing a sense of strong directional force, even though the direct scalar motion is somewhat hidden within the undulations of the melody. In this regard study Ex. 2-7D and E. Several such occurrences are also bracketed in Ex. 2-1A, C, and D.

EXAMPLE 2-7

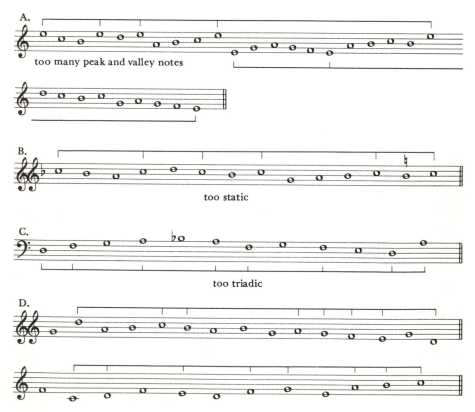

ASSIGNMENT

Using the succession of pitches (without rhythm) in Ex. 2-8, point out any stylistic errors in terms of the previous discussion.

EXAMPLE 2-8

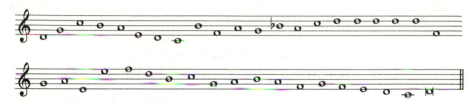

RHYTHMIC CHARACTERISTICS
OF MELODIC LINES

A few general considerations of white-note rhythmic durations may be noted. The larger note values (breves, dotted breves, and dotted semibreves) occur exclusively on strong beats (1 or 3). It is therefore only possible to tie a semibreve to a minim, not the reverse: o.= o ♩ *not* ♩ o. However, tying a semibreve to a breve is permitted: |o|. = |o| o or o |o| (see Ex. 2-9A). Compositions must begin wih values of at least a semibreve or longer (Ex. 2-9B). In the same way, the final note of a piece is always a breve, even if it occurs on the third beat (Ex. 2-9C). It is rare to find a breve followed by a minim (Ex. 2-9D).

Finally, rests must occur on strong beats *only* (1 or 3, but never 2 or 4); consult Ex. 2-9E.

EXAMPLE 2-9

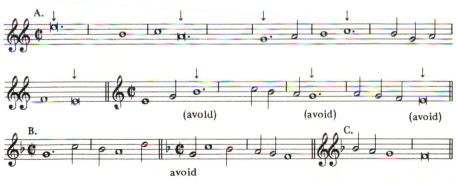

(continues on following pg.)

EXAMPLE 2-9   (*continued*)

rare

avoid

Considering the vocal nature of this music, it is somewhat surprising to find that many authors of contrapuntal texts have failed to comment extensively on the question of text setting. The sacred Latin text, with its interplay of accented and unaccented syllables, is perhaps the primary influence on the rhythm of the individual melodic lines. The following generalities may serve as guidelines in this area.[6] Any white note may carry a syllable of text. The final breve of a composition must be set with a syllable of text; as we shall see later, this also applies in principle to the last note of interior cadences. Accented syllables are usually set with longer note values, regardless of which beat they may fall on. This recalls the basic concept of *agogic* (or quantitative) *accent*. Consult Ex. 2-10.

EXAMPLE 2-10

Palestrina: *Missa Repleatur os meum laude*

Ký- ri- e e- léi- son Ký- rie e- léi- son.

Melismatic passages are normally initiated with an accented syllable and a relatively long duration (Ex. 2-11). There is a strong tendency toward a mixture of syllabic and melismatic setting in this style (see both Ex. 2-11 and 2-13). Extensive *neumatic* text setting (that is, two or three notes per syllable) is somewhat rare.

EXAMPLE 2-11

Palestrina: *Missa Sanctorum meritis*

Á- gnus Dé- i Á- gnus Dé- i.

[6]Both Vincentino and Zarlino laid down certain guidelines for the setting of texts. A summary of Zarlino's ten rules in volume IV of his *Istitutioni harmoniche* (1558) may be found in Samuel P. Rubio, *Classical Polyphony*, tr. by Thomas Riva (Oxford: Basil Blackwell, 1972), pp. 71–76.

The application of the principles noted above results in what Soderlund terms the *microrhythm* of the individual melodic lines.[7] In many cases the irregular recurrence of agogic accents creates a kind of "changing meter" effect, which may be demonstrated by barring the music according to text accents and longer durations. Repetitions of rhythmic figures which suggest a strong metric or "dance-like" feeling are normally avoided. Compare the two versions in Ex. 2-12.

EXAMPLE 2-12

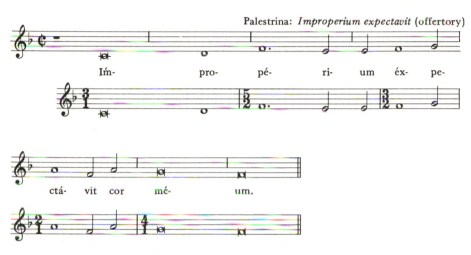

Palestrina: *Improperium expectavit* (offertory)

One may often note a kind of rhythmic acceleration (or "snowballing" effect) in the opening phrase of a composition, in that it may begin with relatively long note values, to be followed by notes of increasingly shorter duration (Ex. 2-13). This statement does not apply to interior themes or phrases, however, where the rhythmic activity is normally greater and more consistent.

EXAMPLE 2-13

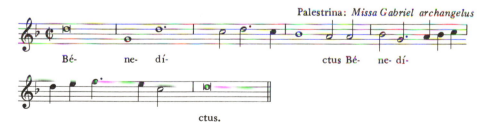

Palestrina: *Missa Gabriel archangelus*

[7]Soderlund, *Direct Approach*, p. 7.

In dividing a given text into separate phrases for musical setting, most composers of this period tended to choose phrases that varied in length from five to fourteen syllables. In some instances the longer phrases are, in turn, subdivided into two shorter thematic ideas of four to eight syllables, which are usually separated by a rest. In such a case it is the second unit that is usually developed more extensively through subsequent reentries. Each recurrence of the initial thematic subject is accompanied by its original text setting. In this regard examine Ex. 2-14.

EXAMPLE 2-14

Palestrina: *Dies sanctificatus* (motet)

Di   es   sán-   cti- fi- cá-   tus   il-   lú- xit nó-

(later)

bis   il- lú- xit   ńo-   bis

As noted previously, the approach to either a final or interior cadence is always by stepwise motion. In the simple (*semplice*) cadence the penultimate note is set with a semibreve (Ex. 2-15A). In the elaborated (*diminuta*) cadence the lower approach consists of the cadence tone (set to a semibreve), followed by the leading tone (with a minim).[8] Several illustrations are given in Ex. 2-15B.

EXAMPLE 2-15

ASSIGNMENT

Study the two passages in Ex. 2-16 and 17, taking into consideration the above discussion. Then, compose two comparable pieces on the same texts in the Mixolydian and Phrygian modes respectively. Observe correct nota-

---

[8]The reason for this rhythmic setting will become clear when two-voice cadences and their attendant suspension formulas are discussed in chapter 3.

tional procedures, including the use of *Mensurstriche*. Then, rebar one of your passages using changing meter signatures, as shown in Ex. 2-12, to illustrate the shifting metric patterns.

EXAMPLE 2-16

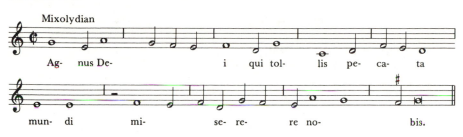

EXAMPLE 2-17

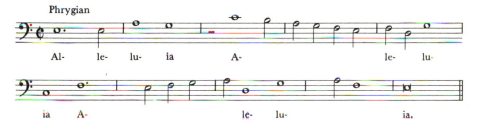

3

Two-Voice Texture with White Notes

Two-voice compositions (often called *bicinia*) are comparatively rare in this period. They tend to appear in separate collections by composers and are often secular or instrumental in nature.[1] Although one may encounter subdivisions of the larger mass movements set in two voices during the late fifteenth century (such as the Crucifixus of the Credo), by the middle of the following century these had given way to three-voice settings. For the time being this chapter will limit the available rhythmic resources to the use of white notes only.

The term *punctum contra punctus*, from which we derive the word counterpoint, originally referred to the *organal* practice of setting a given

[1]Perhaps the best known collection of duets is the set of twenty-four vocal and instrumental pieces by Lassus published under the title *Novae aliquot* (1598). The twelve vocal works (usually referred to as *Cantiones duarum vocum*) may be found in Gustave Soderlund and Samuel Scott, *Examples of Gregorian Chant and Other Sacred Music of the Sixteenth Century* (Englewood Cliffs, NJ: Prentice-Hall, Inc., 1971), pp. 10–33. The remaining twelve instrumental works appear in *Cantiones sine textu*, ed. by Paul Boepple (New York: Music Press Inc., 1942). Other collections of bicinia in modern edition are Eustachio Romano, *Musica duorum*, ed. by Howard Mayer Brown (Chicago: University of Chicago Press, 1978); Vincenzo Galilei, *Contrapunti a due voci*, ed. by Louise Rood (Northampton: Smith College, 1945); Ihan Gero, *Il primo libro de madrigali Italiani*, vol. 1 of *Masters and Monuments of the Renaissance*, ed. by Lawrence Bernstein and James Haar (New York: Broude Brothers Ltd., 1980); Orlando Gibbons, *Fantasias*, ed. by Hannalore Müller (New York: C. F. Peters Corp., 1970); Thomas Morley, *Two Part Canzonets for Voices and Instruments*, ed. by D. H. Boalch (Oxford: G. Ronand, 1950); George Rhaw, *Bicinia gallica et latina*, ed. by von Hulmet Mönkemeyer (New York: C. F. Peters Corp., 1963). Additional vocal duets are included on pp. 33–52 of the Soderlund and Scott anthology cited above.

chant melody with another line either above or below it in similar durations, resulting in a note-against-note (or so-called *first species*) style. The
art of polyphony synonymous with counterpoint (or *canto figurato*, as it was
called in the Late Renaissance), is usually defined as the craft of combining
two or more melodic strands, each with its own characteristic contour and
rhythmic life. As opposed to homophonic texture, in which one melodic
line emerges as the foreground element, in counterpoint the separate
voices coexist on somewhat equal terms. As the ear has difficulty in following two (or more) parts simultaneously, it therefore tends to switch its attention back and forth between the various melodic lines. In order, therefore, to maximize the distinct properties of each voice, it is necessary to
adhere to several basic principles.

1. The parts should be separated spatially, with each assigned to a particular
    pitch range. Although occasional voice-crossing may be tolerated, excessive
    use of this device will result in a confusion of the different melodic strands.
2. Each part should exhibit a distinctive melodic pitch motion and contour.
    Even in the case of *imitation*, where a later voice (or voices) may enter with a
    restatement of the first idea, at any given point the lines should still be me-
    lodically independent. This should result in a mixture of various types of
    motion in the two voices: (1) *similar*, where the parts move in the same direc-
    tion, (2) *contrary*, where they move in opposite directions, and (3) *oblique*,
    where one part is sustained while the other moves against it. An excess of
    similar or parallel motion will negate the contrapuntal process, since the ear
    will tend to elevate one voice to a position of prominence, with an accompa-
    nying intervallic or chordal "thickening." On the other hand, it is just as in-
    correct to rely exclusively on contrary motion.
3. The vertical result of the separate lines should produce harmonic intervals or
    sonorities that are compatible with the stylistic norms under consideration. In
    this period the norm is consonance, with a highly regulated handling of all
    dissonant elements.
4. Finally, the rhythmic characteristics of each part should be distinctive and in-
    dividual from the others. In a sense this is really the lifeblood of polyphony,
    for it is motion through time that activates the pitch succession of the voices.
    The combination of the lines produces a kind of rhythmic complementation,
    in that while one is sustaining, the other is moving. Thus, there is a continual
    interplay of movement that preserves the independence of the voices.

CONSONANT HARMONIC
INTERVALS

Harmonic intervals are always calculated from the lowest sounding voice
part (called the *basso seguente*). The consonant intervals in this period are
the unison, octave, perfect fifth, and all diatonic thirds and sixths. Diatonic
tenths and the perfect twelfth are permitted, although they are somewhat
less frequent. Dissonant intervals, which include seconds, sevenths, and
all diminished and augmented intervals, must be treated and explained in

terms of nonharmonic activity, and as such will be treated later in this chapter.

Those pieces in which both parts start simultaneously begin with either a unison, octave, or perfect fifth. Since in each mode certain initial pitch classes are preferred, it is best to consult Fig. 1-7 before beginning a composition. The first note value must be at least a semibreve in length.

For either final or interior cadences, only the unison or octave is permitted on the last note. As stated previously, it must be approached stepwise in *both* voices (the so-called *clausula vera* or *cadenza perfetta*), resulting in either the movement of a minor third to a unison or a major sixth to an octave. *Musica ficta* is normally assumed with cadential notes on D, G, and A, where a leading tone is necessary. Study the illustrations in Ex. 3-1.

EXAMPLE 3-1

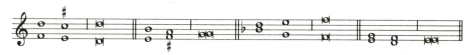

Perfect consonances within the phrase must be handled with care as regards their approach and departure. Unisons are found only on weak beats (2 or 4), and must be approached and left by contrary or oblique motion (see Ex. 3-2A). Octaves may occasionally be found on strong beats, although their excessive use, as in the case of the unison, is discouraged. Their use on weak beats is permitted, and they are also approached and left in the same manner as the unison (see Ex. 3-2B).

EXAMPLE 3-2

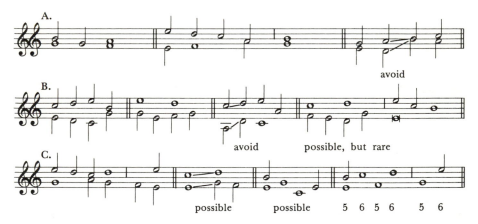

Perfect fifths are usually approached by contrary or oblique motion. In those infrequent cases in which similar motion is employed, one voice must move stepwise while the other voice moves by leap. Perfect fifths on consecutive strong beats are possible, provided an imperfect consonance intervenes. Patterns of successive descending 6-5s are frequently found, producing the fifths on consecutive weak beats. Consult the illustrations in Ex. 3-2C.

As is apparent from the above discussion, parallel perfect intervals are obviously forbidden in this style. Examine those instances shown in Ex. 3-3.

EXAMPLE 3-3

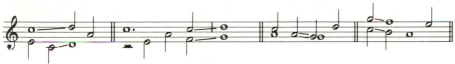

The imperfect consonances (thirds, sixths, and tenths) may be approached and left freely (see Ex. 3-4A). However, more than three consecutive thirds or sixths in similar motion are to be avoided, as the independence of the individual lines will suffer (see Ex. 3-4B).

EXAMPLE 3-4

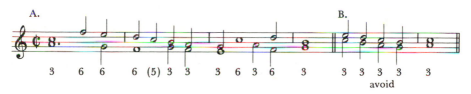

ASSIGNMENTS

Write two-part pieces for either the same or adjacent voices (*cantus-cantus, cantus-altus, tenor-bassus*, etc.). Strive to keep the voices within the range of an octave harmonically, using compound intervals sparingly (never more than a twelfth). Short stretches of voice-crossing are permitted. Study the short piece in Ex. 3-5, which makes exclusive use of consonant intervals. Write in the resulting harmonic intervals, noting the manner in which the perfect intervals are approached and left.

EXAMPLE 3-5

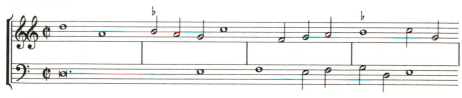

(continues on following pg.)

EXAMPLE 3-5   *(continued)*

Using the following given melody (or *cantus firmus*), write a counter-point both above and below it in one-to-one note values (so-called *first species* or *contrapunto semplice*). Only consonant intervals are permitted. Despite the severe limitations, strive for a good melodic line.[2] Similar motion to fifths is not allowed in first species style.

EXAMPLE 3-6

Write a piece similar to Ex. 3-5 (of six to eight measures), employing only consonant intervals. Choose your own mode and use the following text:

Ré- qui- em ae- tér- nam dó- na é- is, Dó- mi- ne.
(Rest   eternal   give   to us,   Lord)

DISSONANT WHITE NOTES

Only two types of dissonance may be used with minims in two voices texture—passing tones and suspensions.[3] All others involve black notation and will be discussed in chapter 5.

Passing tone minims occur only on weak beats (2 or 4). They may ascend or descend, but the dissonant tones must "pass" against at least a semibreve value (Ex. 3-7A and B). The note opposite the passing dissonance must not be reiterated (Ex. 3-7C), but it can leap, once the passing tone has been resolved (Ex. 3-7D). What is the problem in Ex. 3-7E?

The two-voice suspension is a particularly expressive dissonance as it always falls on a strong beat (1 or 3), a metric position normally reserved for consonance. Suspensions are always prepared by the same previous

---

[2]For several examples of first species see appendix 1.
[3]Second species (2:1) employs only consonance and passing tones, while fourth species makes use of suspensions (see appendix 1).

EXAMPLE 3-7

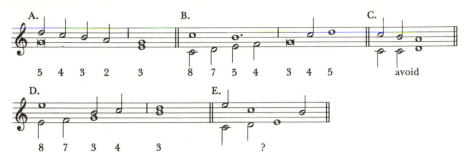

pitch and are resolved downward, stepwise in this style. The suspended dissonance is normally "tied into" from its preparation, producing a white note *syncope* (or *sincopa*) equaling a semibreve in duration ($\sqcup \; \sqcup \; \sqcup$ = $\sqcup$). However, in certain instances of text setting one may find the suspended minim reiterated with a new syllable.

FIGURE 3-1   Three Minims of the Suspension Figure

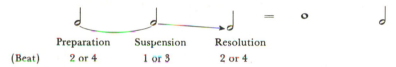

	Preparation	Suspension	Resolution
(Beat)	2 or 4	1 or 3	2 or 4

The most common suspensions in two-voice texture are the 7-6 (in the upper voice) and its inversion the 2-3 (in the lower voice); examine Ex. 3-8A and B. Although it uses the intervals 2-3 Ex. 3-8C shows a typical error; why is it incorrect? The 4-3 (in the upper voice) is possible although somewhat less common; instances of augmented fourths are extremely rare (Ex. 3-8D and E). The 9-8 should be avoided, as its resolution into the empty octave is less than desirable (Ex. 3-8F). In a 7-6 or a 2-3 progression, the voice not involved with the suspension may leap to a consonance (usually a third or sixth respectively) when the suspension resolves, creating a so-called *change of part* (Ex. 3-8G and H). Why is Ex. 3-8I an incorrect suspension?

EXAMPLE 3-8

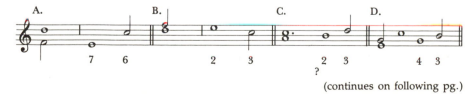

(continues on following pg.)

EXAMPLE 3-8   (*continued*)

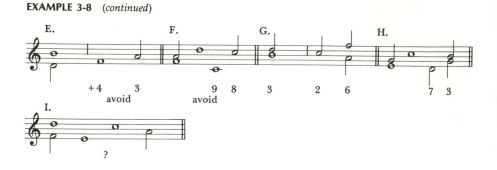

CADENCES

As noted previously, cadences in two voices feature stepwise motion in both parts, either to a unison or octave. Cadences in this period are almost always preceded immediately by either 7-6 suspension, which resolves to the octave, or a 2-3 suspension, which resolves to the unison. Appropriate *musica ficta* will normally be supplied above the resolution of the suspension in those cadences where necessary (C♯-D, F♯-G, or G♯-A in the untransposed modes). The customary Phrygian cadence on E ($^{\text{F-E}}_{\text{D-E}}$), may also appear on A using a B♭ ($^{\text{B♭-A}}_{\text{G-}\ \text{A}}$). The final cadential interval (octave or unison) must fall on a strong beat. At the conclusion of a composition it is possible to cadence on the third beat; in this case the final duration will still be a breve in length. Further discussion involving interior cadences is reserved for chapter 5. Some typical cadential formulas are shown in Ex. 3-9.

EXAMPLE 3-9

ASSIGNMENTS

The following short piece in Ex. 3-10 contains a number of incorrect treatments of dissonant, rhythmic, and melodic procedures. Analyze it first by indicating the harmonic interval occurring on each beat, then circle each error and comment briefly.

EXAMPLE 3-10

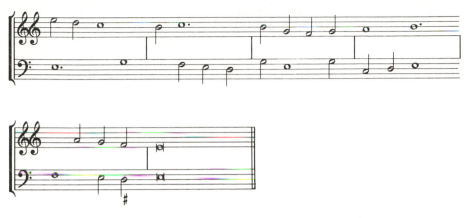

Write a short piece of about ten measures in duration in a mode of your own choice. Use both consonant and dissonant white notes, concluding with a correct cadence for the mode. Try to incorporate several different types of suspensions into the music in addition to passing tones. Use the following text:

Cúm sán- cto Spí- ri- tu, in gló- ri- a Dé- i Pá- tris
(With the holy spirit in the glory of God the Father)

IMITATION IN TWO-VOICE TEXTURE

The use of imitation (or a *point of imitation*) may be considered as the normal procedure at the beginning of sacred polyphonic compositions in this period. In addition, the introduction of new text and thematic material following interior cadences is also usually treated in an imitative fashion. The following remarks, however, refer only to the opening point of imitation in a two-voice piece.

The temporal distance between imitating voices is normally an even number of beats, usually 2, 4, 6, or 8. Virtually all exceptions occur in imitation *per arsin et thesin*, where the distance of one beat may be encountered.

The most common intervals between imitating voices are the octave (*diapason*), the perfect fifth (*diapente*), and the perfect fourth (*diatesseron*); the unison is sometimes found. If the second voice is imitated below the opening theme, the prefix *sub* is added (*subdiapente*). Either voice may begin first. The specific pitch classes chosen to initiate the piece will depend, of course, on the mode employed and may be found in Fig. 1-7.

The use of strict (*legate*) imitation throughout a piece would result in a two-voice *canon* (from the Greek word for rule). This procedure is discussed in chapter 5. Examples of free (or *sciolte*) imitation are more commonly encountered. Here strict imitation is carried on for a few measures and then dropped in favor of simple free counterpoint; in this regard consult Ex. 3-11A. The theorists of the period used the term *fuga* to denote that the intervallic progression of the imitating voice is exactly like that of the opening voice (major second for major second, or minor third for minor third). Thus, the solmization syllables for the imitating parts will remain constant, provided that the imitation takes place at some perfect interval. Note that as a result E-F (Mi-Fa) will be imitated by A-B♭ (also Mi-Fa). This procedure is somewhat synonymous to a *real answer*, although this term is actually more appropriate to the key-oriented baroque period. However, by the middle of the sixteenth century one may occasionally encounter an example of a *tonal answer*, in which an intervallic adjustment has been made in the imitating voice. This usually results from some harmonic consideration.

The initial subject in points of imitation will normally "scan" in one of the three hexachords, allowing a range of C up to A (*naturale*), F up to D (*molle*), or G up to E (*durum*). Examples of mutation are rare. In instances of *fuga* at the fifth above or fourth below, if the original subject scans in the *naturale* or *molle* hexachord, its imitation will appear in the *durum* or *naturale* hexachord respectively. Similarly, in instances of *fuga* at the fifth below or fourth above, if the original subject scans in the *durum* or *naturale* hexachord, its imitation will appear in the *naturale* or *molle* hexachord respectively. Study the excerpts in Ex. 3-11, analyzing each point of imitation for the pitch interval and time distance employed.

EXAMPLE 3-11

ASSIGNMENT

Write two beginning points of imitation in modes of your choice. Employ differing intervals of imitation (perfect intervals) and temporal distances between the voices. Break off the strict imitation after about five or six notes and continue in free counterpoint. Each should be about six or seven measures in length. Conclude with an appropriate cadence.

4

Melodic Writing with Black Notes

Before incorporating black-note values into two-voice polyphony, it is necessary to survey the various idioms that employ these durations in the individual melodic lines. In addition, the problems raised by black notes as regards text setting must be discussed.

The most frequent use of semiminims is found in stepwise motion in the same direction. The single semiminim is encountered only after a dotted minim; the use of semiminim rests ♪ is extremely rare (see Ex. 4-1A). Pairs of stepwise semiminims occur only on weak beats (2 and 4).[1] After a minim, they may either ascend or descend, but following a semibreve or dotted semibreve, they usually descend (Ex. 4-1B). Any number of semiminims may occur after a white note. Examples of three to nine in the same direction are not infrequent (Ex. 4-1C).

EXAMPLE 4-1

[1]For an exception to this rule see Ex. 5-8.

A single semiminim used as a *portamento* (or anticipation figure) occurs on the off-beat of strong beats only (1 or 3). They usually resolve
downward stepwise, although rare examples of ascending patterns may be
encountered (consult Ex. 4-2).

EXAMPLE 4-2

Stepwise semiminims with a change of direction, creating *auxilaries*
(or neighboring tone figures) are common. They generally occur on the off-
beat (of any beat). Instances of the lower auxilary are much more common;
see Ex. 4-3.

EXAMPLE 4-3

Leaps involving black notes are somewhat restricted in their use. One
of the most common figures is that of the *nota cambiata* (or changed note),
which is a melodic idiom frequently found in Renaissance music. In the
fifteenth century it often consisted of only three pitches (Ex. 4-4A), but in
the following century an additional note, ascending stepwise, was added
to counterbalance the downward leap of the third. This device may commence on any beat. Three different rhythmic settings may be encountered;
note that despite the durational changes, the melodic contour remains in-

tact (Ex. 4-4B to D). The so-called "filled-in" *cambiata* is also common (Ex. 4-4E). The idiom is never found in an inverted state (Ex. 4-4F).

EXAMPLE 4-4

Certain restrictions may be mentioned as regards semiminim leaps into or out of white-note values. Leaps to semiminims occur only after a minim (Ex. 4-5A and B). In the case of a single semiminim following a dotted minim, the motion is always downward, with a subsequent change of direction (Ex. 4-5C). After a leap into a white note, the semiminim(s) is always left by contrary motion (Ex. 4-5D to F).

EXAMPLE 4-5

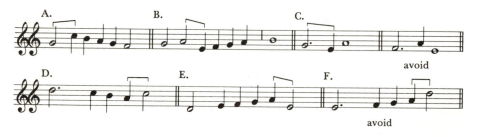

Regarding leaps *within* semiminim passages the so-called "high- and low-note law" may be evoked.[2] Downward leaps generally take place from the beat to the off-beat (Ex. 4-6A), while upward leaps take place from the off-beat to the beat (Ex. 4-6B). Direction is always changed to balance the leap.

EXAMPLE 4-6

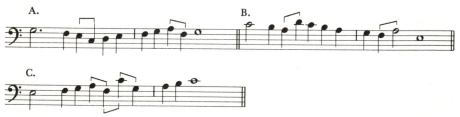

[2]This general rule takes into consideration a great number of specific melodic idioms involving leaps within semiminim passages. Soderlund, in his *Direct Approach*, quotes over twenty-five different examples (see pp. 40–43).

Fusas are found only as stepwise pairs on any off-beat. The two notes are approached and left by stepwise motion; however, upper neighboring figures are not idiomatic (Ex. 4-7).

EXAMPLE 4-7

rare

TEXT SETTING WITH BLACK NOTES

Problems often arise when setting text to passages involving black notes. The following five rules will serve as guides in these instances.

1. When the third from the last syllable of a word is accented (Dó- mi- ne or ex- pec- tá- ti- o) the next-to-last syllable can be carried by a single semiminim (Ex. 4-8A-B). Observe that Ex. 4-8C is correct while Ex. 4-8D is not found in the style.

EXAMPLE 4-8

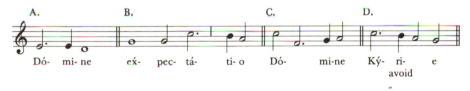

2. A passage of black notes beginning *on* a beat may initiate a syllable, but no change of text is permitted *within* the passage; consult Ex. 4-9.

EXAMPLE 4-9

3. The first white note following a passage of black notes *cannot* carry a syllable. One must wait for the next rhythmic duration (Ex. 4-10).

EXAMPLE 4-10

4.   Neither a pair of *fusas* nor the note following the *fusas* may carry a syllable (Ex. 4-11).

EXAMPLE 4-11

Do-   mi- ne   et   ve-   nit   ve-   nit
         avoid   avoid

5.   Repeated notes, involving either white or black notes, must carry a syllable of text (Ex. 4-12A and B). The only exception is the *portamento,* where the vowel is simply reenunciated (Ex. 4-12C).

EXAMPLE 4-12

qui   tol- lis   pe- ca-   ta   Et   in   Spi-   ri-   tum   San- ctum

pro- no-   bis

Study carefully the melodic lines in Ex. 4-13 and 4-14, recalling the principles discussed that pertain to black notes and their text setting.

EXAMPLE 4-13

Et   ex   Pa-   tre   na-

tus   an-   te   om-

ni- a   sae-   cu-   la.

EXAMPLE 4-14

Ge-   ni- tum non   fa-   ctum   Ge-   ni-

tum non   fa-   ctum.

ASSIGNMENT

Write two melodies about ten measures in duration on the text supplied below. Incorporate various types of black-note idioms and be careful when setting the text. Choose your own modes.

Plé- ni	sunt	cáe-	li	et	tér-	ra	gló-	ri-	a	tú- a.
(Full	are	heaven	and		earth		glory			of your)

In		gló-	ri-	a	Dé-	i	Pá-	tris,	Á- men.
(In			glory	of	God		the	Father,	Amen)

5

Two-Voice Texture with Black Notes

This chapter deals with the use of black-note values in two-part compositions. Extended passages of semiminims are not uncommon in this texture, although as the number of voices begins to increase, the density of black notes usually decreases proportionally. Those rules pertaining to the use of consonance and dissonance with white notes (passing tones and suspensions) are still valid.

If the semiminims are consonant, simply observe the melodic principles established in the previous chapter. In this regard examine Ex. 5-1.

EXAMPLE 5-1

There are a number of specific instances of dissonant black notes that require individual attention:

Unaccented Passing Tones

Unaccented passing tones may occur as semiminims on the *off-beat* of any beat. They may ascend or descend, but must always "pass" against a value of at least a minim. Study Ex. 5-2 carefully, noting all instances of unaccented passing tones.

EXAMPLE 5-2

avoid

Accented Passing Tones

The limitations on the use of accented passing tones are even greater. The accented passing tone normally occurs as the first of a pair of passing semiminims on beats 2 or 4, with the dissonant interval falling *on* the beat. It always resolves downward, stepwise. In this regard examine Ex. 5-3A. The figure in Ex. 5-3B is particularly common near cadences. The only exception to the pairs of semiminims may be encountered in the so-called "filled-in *cambiata*," shown in Ex. 5-3C, where the B fills in the leap from C to A, creating a three-note figure. This is one of the few instances in the style where consecutive dissonant notes may occur (Ex. 5-3D).

EXAMPLE 5-3

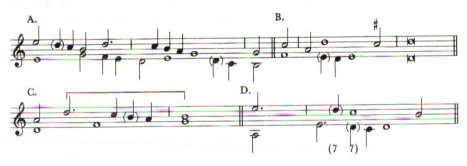

Auxiliaries

Dissonant auxiliaries may occur as *lower* neighboring tones on any off-beat. Their use as upper neighbors, however, is quite rare. Study Ex. 5-4.

EXAMPLE 5-4

avoid

Portamentos

Portamentos (or anticipations) always occur on the off-beats of beats 1 or 3. Although they are normally consonant and feature downward step-wise motion, some exceptions may be noted, as in Ex. 5-5D. Their most frequent use is to ornament a suspension, but strangely enough, they almost never occur at the suspension before a *final* cadence (compare Ex. 5-5A and B). Observe the double *portamento* in semiminims in Ex. 5-5C.

EXAMPLE 5-5

Cambiatas

In the *nota cambiata* the second note of this melodic figure may be either consonant or dissonant (acting as an escape tone). This is the only instance in this style of a nonharmonic tone that involves a leap! The first and third tones of this four-note melodic figure must be consonant. This last note may be either consonant or dissonant; if it is used as a minim passing tone, however, the *cambiata* idiom should begin on a strong beat. Refer to the instances of this figure in Ex. 5-6A and B. Do not confuse the *cambiata* with the resolution of a semiminim suspension, as in Ex. 5-6C.

EXAMPLE 5-6

Fusas

Fusas are invariably found in pairs. They are most often employed to ornament suspensions, particularly at cadences. In the case of a 2-3 or 4-3 suspension, the second fusa will act as a miniature dissonant neighbor. If the first fusa is dissonant (either a passing tone or neighbor), the motion is always downward. Several typical examples may be noted in Ex. 5-7.

EXAMPLE 5-7

Suspensions

Although the suspension is more properly a white-note device, there are a number of black-note idioms often closely associated with it. Three have been alluded to above: an accented passing note in relation to its preparation (Ex. 5-3B), and the ornamentation of the suspended note with either a *portamento* (Ex. 5-5A) or a pair of fusas (Ex. 5-7). Often the preparation is preceded by a pair of *ascending* semiminims, as in Ex. 5-8, one of the few instances where this idiom is found on a strong beat and in an ascending form.

EXAMPLE 5-8

The following three examples will serve as a summary of the foregoing discussion. They should be thoroughly analyzed, with particular attention paid to the treatment of black notes as regards consonance and dissonance. Ex. 5-9 represents a florid counterpoint set over a *cantus firmus* (or *soggetto*). It is equivalent to fifth species, although the theorists of that period employed the term *contrapunto diminuto*.[1]

EXAMPLE 5-9

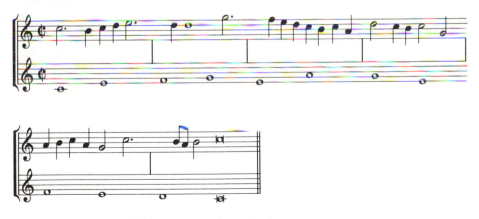

[1]For examples of fifth species see appendix 1.

EXAMPLE 5-10

EXAMPLE 5-11

ASSIGNMENTS

Examine Ex. 5-12, circling and commenting on any incorrect use of melodic idioms, handling of dissonance, rhythm, setting of text, etc. Do not be alarmed at the large number of errors; there are over twenty!

EXAMPLE 5-12

Write an example of free counterpoint (no text or imitation) for two voices, of eight to ten measures in duration, employing various types of black-note idioms. Try to include at least one example of an accented passing tone, *portamento*, *cambiata*, and eighth notes.

Write a short piece of about ten measures in length incorporating all of the various contrapuntal resources discussed thus far. Use the following text, and begin with imitation at the perfect fifth.

Dí- es	śan-	cti-	fi-	cá- tus	il-	lú-	xit	nó-	bis.
(Day		most holy			enlighten				us)

6

Other Aspects
of Two-Voice
Texture

This chapter concludes the presentation of those stylistic characteristics pertaining to two-voice texture. The topics explored here include those of double counterpoint, canonic writing, general structural considerations, interior cadences and phrases, and techniques encountered in instrumental composition.

DOUBLE COUNTERPOINT

Invertible counterpoint in two-voice texture (*double counterpoint*) involves the textural switching of parts, so that the original upper voice becomes the lower and vice versa $\left(\begin{smallmatrix} \text{upper} \\ \text{lower} \end{smallmatrix}\times\right)$. Thus, each voice has a double function— as an upper part or as the bass. This device is frequently encountered in baroque fugue technique, where the original counterpoint is retained with subsequent reentries of the subject. However, in the Renaissance, composers seem content to write new counterpoints to accompany reentries, so that this device occurs only sporadically.

Of the three basic categories listed below, counterpoint at the twelfth is most frequent. The tables included show the resultant intervallic inversions; remember that a unison is 1, not 0. Normally, the harmonic range of the particular type of double counterpoint under consideration is not exceeded. If this does occur, the voices will cross, as denoted by negative numbers in the tables.

In double counterpoint at the octave, the consonant and dissonant properties of the intervals remain basically constant under inversion (consult Fig. 6-1).[1]

FIGURE 6-1   Intervallic Table for Double Counterpoint at the Octave

-3	-2		1	2	3	4	5	6	7	8		9	10
10	9		8	7	6	5	4	3	2	1		-2	-3

The sole exception is the perfect fifth, which inverts into a dissonant fourth. For this reason all perfect fifths must be treated as though they were actually dissonant intervals, such as passing tones or suspensions. Ex. 6-1 illustrates several such instances.

EXAMPLE 6-1

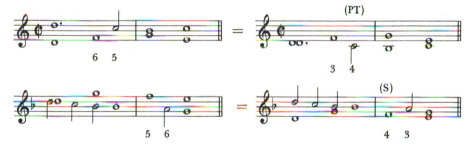

In his five-voice motet, *Alleluia tulerunt,* Palestrina continually pairs two short melodic fragments in contrapuntal association, which results in several instances of double counterpoint at the octave. Two such excerpts are shown in Ex. 6-2.

EXAMPLE 6-2

Palestrina: *Alleluia tulerunt*

[1]Counterpoint at the double octave (or fifteenth) is also possible; the inversional relations between consonant and dissonant intervals are identical with those at the simple octave, although compound intervals are employed. Such instances are somewhat rare.

The use of double counterpoint at the tenth is somewhat rare. Here one must be on continual guard against similar motion in thirds or sixths, as these invert into octaves and fifths respectively. Study Fig. 6-2 for the various inversional properties of the intervals.

FIGURE 6-2   Intervallic Table for Double Counterpoint at the Tenth

-3	-2		1	2	3	4	5	6	7	8	9	10		11	12
12	11		10	9	8	7	6	5	4	3	2	1		-2	-3

The brief imitative excerpt in Ex. 6-3 is taken from part three of *Le Istitutioni harmoniche*, Zarlino's monumental treatise on the art of counterpoint.

EXAMPLE 6-3

Zarlino: *Le Istitutioni harmoniche* (part 3)

Examples of double counterpoint at the twelfth may be noted with some frequency in two-voice compositions. In the table in Fig. 6-3, note that the 2-3 suspension inverts into a compound 4-3 (actually 11-10) suspension, and vice versa.

FIGURE 6-3   Intervallic Table for Double Counterpoint at the Twelfth

-3	-2		1	2	3	4	5	6	7	8	9	10	11	12		13	14
14	13		12	11	10	9	8	7	6	5	4	3	2	1		-2	-3

Here the problem interval is the sixth, which inverts into the dissonant seventh. As a consequence, any such instances of a harmonic sixth must be treated as though it were a correctly prepared and resolved dissonance. Two methods of its correct occurrence are illustrated in Ex. 6-4, first as a passing tone and then as a 7-6 suspension.

EXAMPLE 6-4

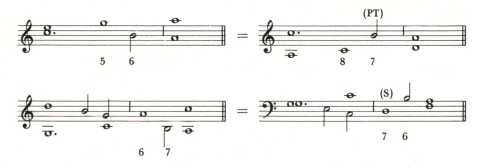

When employing some types of double counterpoint, such as that at the twelfth, the spatial displacement of one of the voices may create range problems. For this reason it is often advantageous to *transpose* the pitch level of both parts. When inverting and transposing at the same time it is helpful to employ the use of a "magic number," which is always one more than the mode of inversion; for example, in the case of double counterpoint at the twelfth, 13 (12 + 1). In double counterpoint at the octave, for instance, if one wishes to transpose the lower part a fifth higher during inversion, then the other voice will be placed a fourth lower, or $5\uparrow + 4\downarrow = 9$ (or 8+1). In counterpoint at the twelfth the most frequently used transposition level is $8\uparrow + 5\downarrow$ or $5\uparrow + 8\downarrow = 13$ (12 + 1). This is demonstrated in Ex. 6-5.

EXAMPLE 6-5

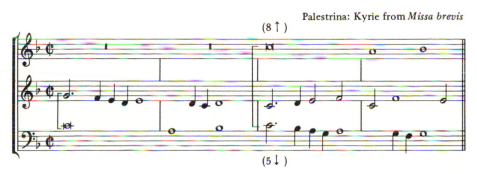

Palestrina: Kyrie from *Missa brevis*

The following passage represents one of the earliest examples of double counterpoint at the twelfth found in a theoretical treatise. As the inversional process is not quoted in the original source, a realization is given in Ex. 6-6, using 8 + 5 (the soprano drops an octave, while the bass rises a fifth). Note the curious dissonance in the last measure.

EXAMPLE 6-6

Vincentino: *L'antico musica* Vol. 4

ASSIGNMENTS

How many different ways will the passage in Ex. 6-7 invert, using counterpoint at the octave, tenth, or twelfth? Write out each workable version, disregarding unisons on strong beats.

EXAMPLE 6-7

Write a short passage of about eight measures duration using counterpoint at the twelfth. No text is necessary. Employ two examples of "correct" sixths. You may wish to transpose the parts if the range becomes a problem upon inversion. Be sure to write out the original voices first and then recopy them showing the inversional process.

CANONIC WRITING IN TWO
VOICES

The *canon* is a composition in which the other part (or parts) is derived from the original voice by *rule* (hence the Greek word *kanon*). This usually results in a polyphonic piece employing strict imitation throughout its duration. It was termed a *fuga* (or imitation) in strict style (*legate*) by theorists of the period. The frequent use of canonic technique had declined by the middle of the sixteenth century, being more typical of the previous century. As a result, examples of complete two-voice canons are relatively infrequent, although the use of shorter sections of canonic imitation within the framework of a bicinium may be noted.[2] The leading voice (*guida*) is usually imitated by the follower voice (*consequente*) at the perfect intervals of the unison, octave, fourth, or fifth, either above or below.[3] A two-voice canon is referred to as a "2 in 1" canon, since only the *guida* part is customarily notated. The *consequente* is then realized once the imitative interval and distance are known. The *presa* (𝄉) is employed to denote where the *consequente* enters temporally, while the *coronata* (⌒) indicates where the *consequente* would cease imitating. In the realization of a canon, appropriate *musica ficta* must sometimes be inserted for cadential formulas or to correct the tritone. The study of three-voice canons will be taken up in chapter 11.

ASSIGNMENTS

Realize Zarlino's two-voice canon in Ex. 6-8 by copying out both parts. Note the clever manner in which the composer is able to set up an interior cadence within the context of the strict imitation (see measures 12-13). How does the given *guida* voice tell us which interval of imitation to use?

Occasionally one may find examples of various contrapuntal devices employed in canonic technique. In a canon *per motu contrario* the *consequente* is a mirror (or melodic inversion) of the *guida* throughout.[4]

In *crab* (*cancrizans*) and *prolation* (or *mensuration*) canons, both voices begin simultaneously. The former features strict retrograde motion be-

---

[2] In this regard analyze measures 9-17 and 22-25 of Ex. 7-2. The practice of embedding a two-part canon within a texture of four or five voices is fairly common. Perhaps the outstanding example of this procedure may be found in Palestrina's *Missa Repleatur os meum laude*. For each successive section or movement the intervallic and temporal distance between the two voices decreases progressively: Kyrie I (at the octave and eight semibreves); Christe (at the seventh and seven semibreves); Kyrie II (at the sixth and six semibreves); etc.

[3] One will also encounter the Latin terms for the leader (*dux*) and follower (*comes*) voices.

[4] In this form of imitation the intervallic relations between the *rectus* and *inversus* voices will vary unless the axis note is D.

EXAMPLE 6-8

Zarlino: *Le Istitutioni harmoniche* (part 3)

tween the parts (⇋)[5], while the latter involves some proportional rhythmic relationship of one voice to another.[6]

Ex. 6-9 quotes a brief, two-voice prolation canon from Josquin's *L'Homme armé* mass. Note the double meter-signature; in cases of this nature the ¢ denotes the original notated version, while the C indicates that the *consequente* is to be realized in double note values, or a relationship of 2 to 1. The tied breves in measures 9-10 were notated as a *longa* in the original score. Note the *portamento* occurring on a weak beat in measure 13. Realize this canon, copying out both parts on a two-voice score.

EXAMPLE 6-9

Josquin: Benedictus *(Missa L'Homme armé)*

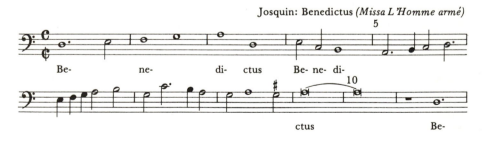

Be-   ne-   di-   ctus   Be- ne- di-

ctus   Be-

[5]For an example of this device see Ex. 12-6.

[6]The most famous exploitation of mensuration is found in Ockeghem's *Missa Prolationum.*

ne- di-   ctus Be-   ne- di-   ctus.

ASPECTS OF STRUCTURE
IN VOCAL TWO-VOICE
COMPOSITIONS

The musical structure of a two-voice piece is determined largely by its text. After the overall text has been partitioned into separate phrases, each successive new phrase is then given a different thematic idea, normally presented in imitation. Once the strict imitative process is dropped, the rest of the phrase proceeds in free counterpoint. Reentries of the initial motive are always accompanied with its original text setting. The phrase will usually conclude with a well-defined cadence although exceptions to this practice may be encountered. The same procedure is then repeated for the following phrases until the piece eventually concludes. The resultant "form" might thus be termed "sectional through-composition." One possible layout is given in Fig. 6-4, using the text of the *Agnus Dei*.

Interior phrases generally exhibit greater rhythmic activity in their associated thematic ideas as compared with the opening measures of a piece. They may begin with a semibreve, dotted minim, or even just a minim, and commonly commence on a weak beat (2 or 4). The later phrases usually contain more instances of thematic reentries. A thematic reentry will normally appear after a rest, either one or two beats in duration. A theme may reenter any number of times, with various intervallic and temporal distances, which often results in a kind of thematic "development." The text setting, note values, and at least the first four pitches of the theme are retained with each reentry. If it begins with a dotted or simple semibreve, the reentry may omit a minim in duration (o· = ▬ o or o = ▬ ♩). Sequences involving thematic restatements and even the use of *stretto* (compressed temporal imitation) are frequently encountered.

FIGURE 6-4 Sectional Through-composed Form Using Agnus Dei Text

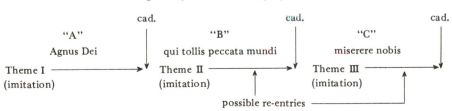

ASSIGNMENT

Analyze Ex. 7-2 in chapter 7 as regards the structural relationship of the piece to its text. Note the lengths of the various phrases, imitative procedures, and cadences.

It is important that the interior cadences of a composition do not unduly interrupt the rhythmic flow of the music. Instances of interior cadences concluding with a breve are somewhat rare (see Ex. 6-10). Not all interior cadences are "structural," in that they conclude a phrase of text, since examples of cadential formulas may be observed within a phrase.

EXAMPLE 6-10

Sometimes the cadencing voice *not* involved with the suspension dissonance may conclude with only a minim, and then immediately initiate the theme of the next phrase, as in Ex. 6-11A. More frequently, however, this part may actually rest at the point of the cadential unison or octave and then begin the new phrase one or two beats later (Ex.6-11B). The suspended voice of the cadence, however, will *always* resolve upward, usually to a semibreve. Theorists of the period termed this technique an "interrupted" cadence (*cadenza sfuggita*).[7] Several instances were shown in Ex. 6-11C.

One may occasionally find an exception to the standard 7-6 or 2-3 cadence formula. Several instances are given in Ex. 6-12, although bear in mind that their occurrence is rare.

---

[7]Soderlund employs the term *hocket* cadence, although it is better not to evoke this medieval device (see p. 56 of his *Direct Approach*).

EXAMPLE 6-11

Lassus: *Cantiones duarum vocum*

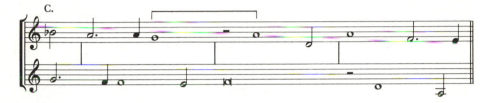

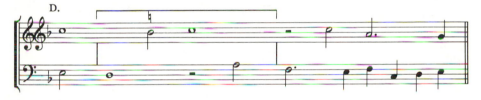

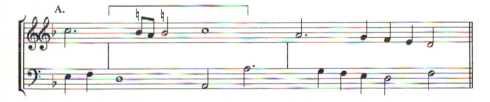

EXAMPLE 6-12

ASSIGNMENTS

In light of the above discussion, study the last phrase (*in nomine Domini*) from two settings of the Benedictus by Lassus. Note any examples of interrupted cadences. As regards Ex. 6-13, what type of invertible counterpoint is employed during the course of the last phrase? Observe the use of thematic sequence a step lower in measures 12-15.

EXAMPLE 6-13

Lassus: Benedictus (*Missa ad Imitationem moduli Iager*)

The movement quoted in Ex. 6-14 is unusual in that roughly four-fifths of the piece is devoted to the last phrase setting. Analyze the various temporal distances and intervallic relations employed in the imitation of the subsequent reentries.

EXAMPLE 6-14

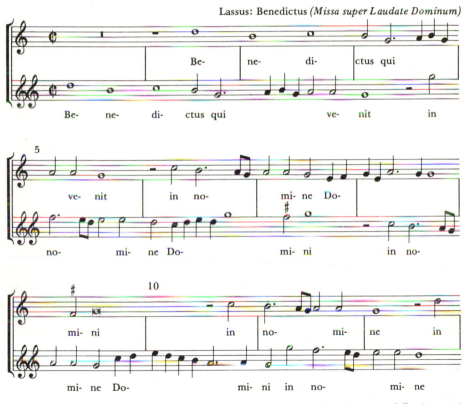

Lassus: Benedictus *(Missa super Laudate Dominum)*

(continues on following pg.)

EXAMPLE 6-14   *(continued)*

As a final project in two-voice writing compose a piece of twenty to thirty measures using the text below. The work should fall into three distinct phrases. Once the mode, initial tones, and interior cadence tones have been chosen, work out such questions as phrase proportion, text repetition, thematic reentries, possible use of interrupted cadences, etc.

Crú- ci-	fí-	xus	e-	tí-	am	pro	nó-	bis,	sub	Pón- tio
(He was crucified		also				for		us,	under	Pontius

Pi-	lá-	to	pás- sus,	et	se-	púl-	tus	ést.
Pilate			he suffered	and		buried		was)

INSTRUMENTAL WRITING IN TWO-VOICE TEXTURE

While the contrapuntal techniques found in instrumental media correspond basically with those of vocal writing, certain deviations, particularly in the area of rhythmic treatment, may be noted. In Ex. 6-15 are two pages excerpted from the part books for the twelve instrumental pieces in Lassus' *Novae aliquot*. The parts illustrated are those for Duet No. 13 of the collection.

The type of printing employed here is called *single impression*, in that the music is put together with individual bits of movable type, each of which consists of a single note or symbol on the staff. Several kinds of rests may be noted: semibreve ▬, minim ▬, and semiminim ⌐. Some instances

EXAMPLE 6-15 *Cantus* and *Bassus* partbooks—Duet no. 13 from Lassus: *Novae aliquot*

of *music ficta* have been inserted by the composer; others may have to be supplied by the performer. Observe the use of the *custos* at the end of each line, which indicates the first note on the succeeding staff.

ASSIGNMENT

Make a modern full score of this piece for two flutes, transposing the parts an octave higher; note that the *cantus* voice employs a treble clef. Be careful to observe the printed rests. Then, analyze the duet for the following points: (1) use of semiminims and fusas, (2) rhythmic treatment of suspensions, (3) cadential points, and (4) motivic treatment and imitation. Do you find many problems with *music ficta*? If possible, perform the piece in class, using a fairly brisk tempo.

7

Examples of Two-Voice Compositions for Analysis

The following six pieces, consisting of complete movements by various composers of the Renaissance, will serve to furnish the student with examples of two-voice texture for subsequent analysis. Each should be studied carefully in light of the discussion in the previous chapters. A few comments precede each work.

EXAMPLE 7-1 Zarlino: from *Le Istitutioni harmoniche* (1558), part three.

This composition falls into three sections, each based on the treatment of thematic material. Note the reentries in the last two sections, with some tonal imitation or modified subjects. There is no text in the original.

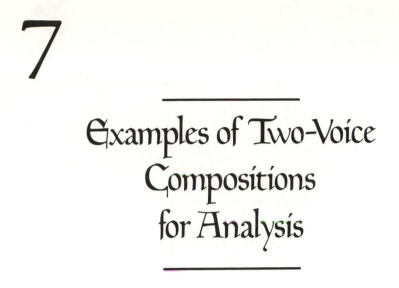

(continues on following pg.)

EXAMPLE 7-1   (*continued*)

EXAMPLE 7-2 Lassus: "Sicut rosa," duet no. 12 from *Novae aliquot* (1598).

The structure, cadences, tonal motion, thematic relationships, and lengths of phrases suggest a kind of overall arch-like form. Compare the double thematic presentation of the opening phrase (what device is employed?) with that of the last phrase. Note the picturesque word painting on the word *florem*.

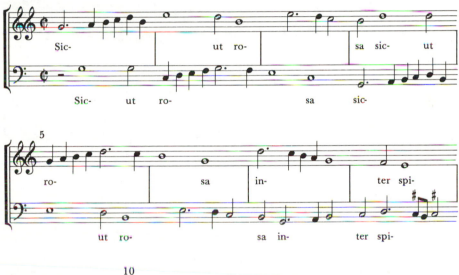

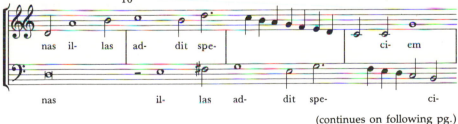

(continues on following pg.)

EXAMPLE 7-2 (*continued*)

vi- ta-   lem dat o-   do-   rem.

lem dat   o- do-   rem.

Sic- ut ro- sa in- ter spi- nas il- las ad- dit spe- ci- em,
(As a rose among thorns to them adds its beauty,

Sic re- nu- stat su- am Vir- go Ma- ri- a pro- ge- ni- em,
So brings the Virgin Mary her descendent,

Ger- mi- na- vit e- nim flo- rem qui vi- ta- lem dat o- do- rem.
He sprouts a flower which living gives a fragrance.)

EXAMPLE 7-3 Josquin: Benedictus from the *Missa Pange lingua* (c. 1514).

Although this setting of the Benedictus belongs more properly to the previous century, the writing adheres in general to the principles discussed before. Nevertheless, a number of minor exceptions do appear; analyze the piece carefully in regards to these stylistic deviations. The opening section is noteworthy for its alternation of antiphony-like phrases. Study measures 38-43, where a large threefold sequence unfolds.

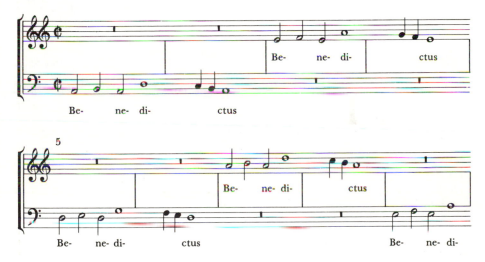

(continues on following pg.)

EXAMPLE 7-3   (*continued*)

Be- ne- di- ctus qui ve- nit in no- mi- ne Do- mi- ni.
(Blessed who comes in the name of the Lord.)

EXAMPLE 7-4　Caspar Othmayr: *Bicinia sacra* (1547?).

Caspar Othmayr (1515 1553) was among the first generation of German Protestant composers in the Late Renaissance. This little bicinium is one of the earliest contrapuntal settings of *Ein feste Burg,* employing Luther's famous tune as a kind of elaborated *cantus firmus* in the lower voice. Do all of the cadences employ the customary suspension formula?

Erd' ist nicht seins- glei- chen.

Erd' ist nicht seins- glei- chen.

Ein fe- ste Burg ist un- ser Gott, ein gu- te Wehr und Waf- fen.
(A mighty fortress is our God, a good defense and weapon.

Der al- te bö- se Feind, mit Ernst er's jetzt meint.
The old evil foe, with earnest he now purposes.

Gross Macht und viel List sein grau- sam Rü- stung ist.
Great power and much craft his cruel armor is.

Auf Erd' ist nicht seins- glei- chen.
On earth is not his equal.)

EXAMPLE 7-5 Vincenzo Galilei: Duet from *Fronimo* (1568).

This example of instrumental writing by the father of the famous astronomer does not divide into short, well-defined phrases with their usual points of imitation and cadences. Observe the interesting handling of suspensions throughout this piece, and the numerous instances of changes of parts.

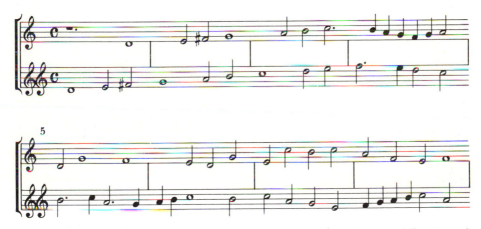

(continues on following pg.)

EXAMPLE 7-5   *(continued)*

EXAMPLE 7-6   Thomas Morley: "Lo, Here Another Love," no. 6 from *Canzonets to Two Voices* (1595).

Although this is obviously a secular work, the compositional technique coincides remarkably well with the principles of two-voice sacred writing. A word about the rhythmic notation: many of the secular pieces in England during this period employ the semiminim as the unit of "beat," rather than the minim. For the sake of analysis, consider all the note values as being doubled. Observe that measures 1-9 = 10-18, and 18-33 = 33-48 approximately, with the voices switched, although no double counterpoint is involved, thus forming a large, repeated two-part form. The text setting is interesting; note the harmonic tritone in measure 47. This is probably best thought of as an implied three-voice cadence formula, which will be discussed in chapter 9.

(continues on following pg.)

EXAMPLE 7-6   (*continued*)

8

Three-Voice
Texture
with White Notes

Although three-voice texture is by no means the norm of the period, numerous examples may be encountered.[1] They usually occur in short responses, offertories, motets, in certain sections of the Credo, and particularly in the Benedictus of the Ordinary of the Mass. The examination of three-part compositions introduces the student to the possibilities of harmony and full triadic textures.

HARMONIC RESOURCES

Vertical sonorities or "chords" in the Late Renaissance were treated as a superposition of consonant intervals above the lowest sounding voice. Two basic categories of harmonic entities are possible. The examples provided will employ C as the given *bassus* pitch.

The first group includes those sonorities containing three different pitch classes with no doubling. As Ex. 8-1 illustrates, these are equivalent in modern terminology to major or minor triads in root position $\frac{5}{3}$ (Ex. 8-1A) and first inversion $\frac{6}{3}$ (Ex. 8-1B). The $\frac{6}{4}$ (second inversion) is not possible because of the relation of the dissonant fourth with the *bassus*. The wide spacing shown in the last chord of each category is relatively uncommon.

---

[1] There are some twenty-seven examples of three-voice polyphony cited in Soderlund and Scott, *Examples of Gregorian Chant*, pp. 57–123.

EXAMPLE 8-1

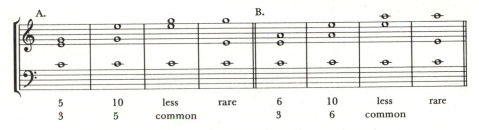

As Ex. 8-2 A through D illustrate, one of the tones is now doubled at the octave. The *bassus* voice is usually the doubled tone, with an included perfect fifth, third, or sixth (as in Ex. 8-2A through C); doublings of the upper voice at the octave are somewhat rare (Ex. 8-2D).

EXAMPLE 8-2

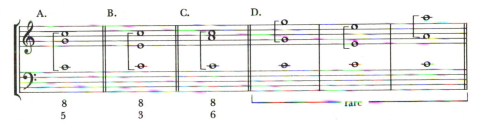

Doubling at the unison is also possible, as shown in Ex. 8-3.

EXAMPLE 8-3

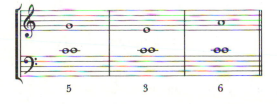

The sonorities used at the openings or conclusions of three-voice compositions are limited in number. The most typical initial chords are given in Ex. 8-4A. As we shall see in the consideration of final cadences, most pieces close with either a doubled octave or unison (Ex. 8-4B), although some cadences will include the sonorities shown in Ex. 8-4C.

Because of the presence of the tritone, diminished triads appear only in $^6_3$ (first inversion), so that the dissonant interval occurs between upper voices rather than in relation to the lower part (Ex. 8-5). The use of augmented triads, also in $^6_3$, are very rare in sacred style, and will be dis-

EXAMPLE 8-4

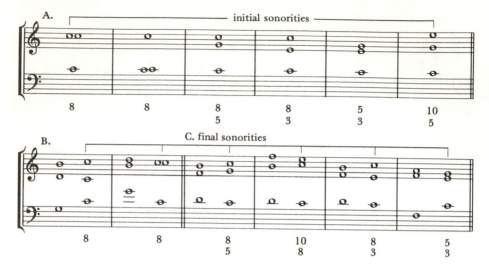

cussed, in connection with somewhat exotic harmonic practices, in chapter 21.

EXAMPLE 8-5

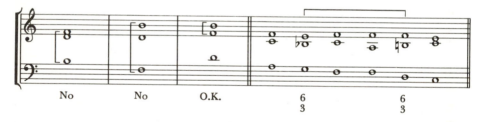

Raised *musica ficta* (C♯, F♯, and G♯ in the untransposed modes) are never doubled. Doubling can occur in the case of B♭. The B minor triad is avoided, as F♯ is not used to correct the tritone. Although *musica ficta* is usually reserved for cadential points, it may sometimes be employed for more purely "coloristic" purposes, thereby extending the range of available harmonic resources (A C♯ E in place of A C E).[2] The total vocabulary of three-note sonorities, disregarding doubling and spacing, is given in Ex. 8-6. For the transposed modes, these would be raised a perfect fourth.

---

[2]Further discussion on "coloristic" harmony may be found under Familiar Style in chapter 13.

EXAMPLE 8-6

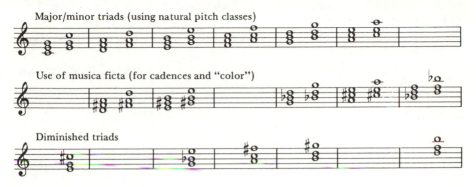

VOICE-LEADING BETWEEN CONSONANT SONORITIES

The following suggestions will help the student to realize the principles of voice-leading between the individual voices of consonant sonorities. Generally write for adjacent voice parts (*cantus, altus, tenor,* or *altus, tenor, bassus,* or even two *cantus* parts and an *altus*). Strive to keep the spacing between the voices fairly close, particularly in the upper parts. The total intervallic span should rarely exceed a perfect twelfth. Even the crossing of voices is permissible for short stretches. Strive for as complete a triadic texture as possible, although the voice-leading will, of necessity, produce sonorities with doubled notes, especially at cadences. The harmonic considerations should not distract from the task of creating good melodic lines. Do not worry about the resultant "chord progressions" at present. At times they may sound quite "functional," although there is usually little sense of harmonic movement in terms of common-practice tonal procedures. Let the *lines* create the harmony.

The approach to perfect intervals must still be handled with care. Unisons are now permitted as doubled notes on any beat, but they must be approached and left by contrary or oblique motion (Ex. 8-7A). Parallel unisons, octaves, and fifths are forbidden. Interestingly enough, the device of voice-crossing may sometimes be employed to prevent parallel fifths between the same voices, although the total harmonic effect still retains the parallels (Ex. 8-7B). Extended passages of consecutive stepwise $^6_3$s (first inversions), known as *fauxbourdon* technique, are not particularly common during this period, although some examples may be found (Ex. 8-7C). The resulting parallel fourths are permissible; however, the use of compound thirds ($^{10}_6$) will create parallel fifths between the upper parts (Ex. 8-7D). Stepwise successions of $^{5-6}_{3-3}$ or its reverse $^{6-5}_{3-3}$ (usually referred to as 5-6 or 6-5) may be found as a means of staggering the parallel fifths (Ex. 8-7E and F). In similar motion to fifths (so-called *direct fifths*) one of the voices must move stepwise while the other leaps (Ex. 8-7G). Direct octaves are somewhat rare; when they do occur, the voice-leading described above is in effect (Ex. 8-7H).

Finally, avoid having all the voices moving or leaping in the same direction (Ex. 8-7I).

EXAMPLE 8-7

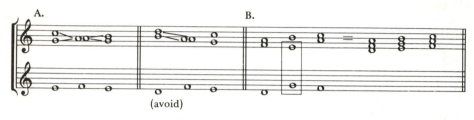

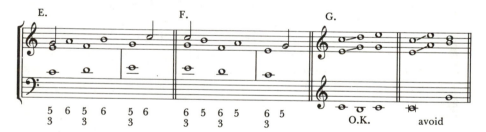

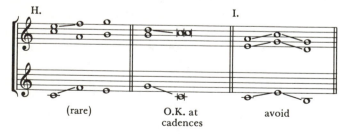

ASSIGNMENTS

Using the following *cantus firmus* as the *bassus* voice (Ex. 8-8), write an example of note-against-note counterpoint (or first species). Strive for good melodic lines and full triadic textures. The penultimate sonority will be a diminished triad on B in first inversion. For a similar example see appendix 1.

EXAMPLE 8-8

(Ionian)

Study the short piece in Ex. 8-9, which employs only consonant combinations in various white-note durations. Analyze each sonority for its intervallic content. Then write a passage of comparable length on the following text:

| Haéc | | dí- | es | quam | fé- | cit | Dó- | mi- | nus. |
| (This is | | the day | | which | has made | | the Lord. | | |

| É- | xul- | té- | mus | et | laé- | te- | mur | in | é- | a. |
| Let us exult | | | | and | be glad | | | in | | it.) |

EXAMPLE 8-9

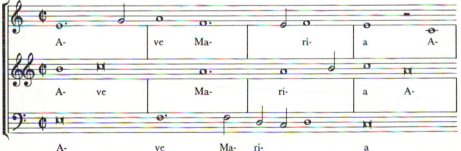

DISSONANCE WITH WHITE NOTES

As in the case of two-voice texture, only minim passing tones and suspensions are permitted.[3]

The passing dissonance (on beats 2 or 4) is always computed against the lowest voice, unless that part becomes a passing tone itself. As in two-voice writing, the minim passing tones must move against at least a consonant semibreve in duration. Single passing tones are very common. They may ascend or descend (Ex. 8-10A). Double passing tones in thirds, sixths, and in contrary motion are permitted (Ex. 8-10B). The third voice may leap in minims against the passing tone and its stationary note, provided that the leap is consonant with *both* the passing tone and the other part. Note in Ex. 8-10C that the C makes a passing tone with the *bassus;* the leap to the F makes a consonant interval with both the C and sustaining D.

Why is Ex. 8-10D incorrect?

EXAMPLE 8-10

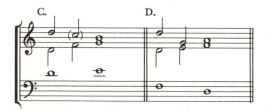

The number of possible suspensions increases in three-voice texture. As there may be several intervallic relations above the lowest voice in addition to the suspension itself, it is often more meaningful to refer to the vertical combination at the point of suspension by indicating $\frac{5}{4}\frac{-}{3}$ or $\frac{6}{4}\frac{-}{3}$ instead of simply 4-3. For the sake of comparison, all the suspensions in the following examples are placed on the first beat, although obviously they may also occur on beat 3 as well. The various categories of suspensions are listed in

---

[3]The two remaining instances of white-note dissonance, the $\frac{6}{5}$ and consonant fourth, are discussed in chapter 9.

terms of their overall relative frequency. Within each group, the more common idioms are discussed first.[4]

The 4-3 is perhaps the most common family of three-voice suspensions. The $\frac{5}{4}$ (Ex. 8-11A) and the $\frac{6}{4}$ (with two forms of resolution in Ex. 8-11B and C) are more frequent than the weaker $\frac{8}{4}$ (Ex. 8-11D). The third voice or the *bassus* may leap, upon the resolution of the suspension, although the doubling of the resolution note on the next beat is rare (Ex. 8-11E and F). One may even note a rare instance of a $\frac{4}{3}\frac{3}{2}$ with the resolution occurring at the point of suspension; however, the interval between the upper voices is almost always a major second (Ex. 8-11G).

EXAMPLE 8-11

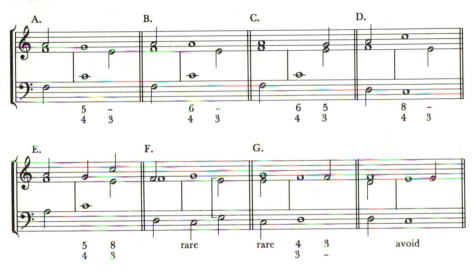

The various types of 7-6 suspensions are possible in the following order of occurence: $\frac{7}{3}$, $\frac{8}{7}$ and $\frac{7}{5}$. Note that the third voice of the $\frac{7}{5}$ must move, upon the resolution of the suspension, in order to avoid a dissonance with the other upper part. An occasional change of bass is even possible. Consult the illustrations in Ex. 8-12.

There are four possible bass or 2-3 suspensions: $\frac{4}{2}$, $\frac{5}{2}$, $\frac{6}{2}$, and $\frac{9}{2}$. The first two examples are the normal forms (Ex. 8-13A through D); note their resolution to either a root-position or first-inversion triad, sometimes through voice-crossing. The final two idioms are given to complete the family of bass suspensions; both are rare (Ex. 8-13E and F).

---

[4]This listing by frequency is based on the study by John Hanson of the three-voice works of Palestrina; see his "Enumeration of Dissonance in the Masses of Palestrina," *College Music Symposium*, 23/1 (Spring 83), pp. 50–64.

EXAMPLE 8-12

EXAMPLE 8-13

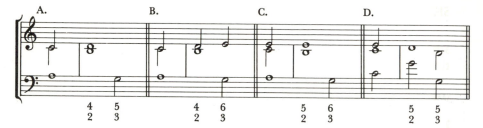

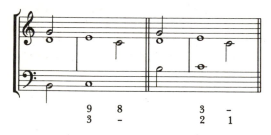

The 9-8 and 2-1 suspensions are only infrequently encountered. The more common types ($\frac{9}{3}$ and $\frac{3}{2}$) are illustrated in Ex. 8-14.

EXAMPLE 8-14

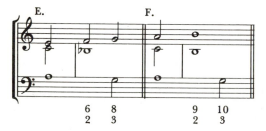

Two double suspensions may be found on occasion. They are the $\frac{7}{4}\frac{6}{3}$ and the $\frac{9}{4}\frac{8}{3}$. The $\frac{9}{7}\frac{8}{6}$ form, curiously enough, is not encountered in the style. Consult Ex. 8-15.

EXAMPLE 8-15

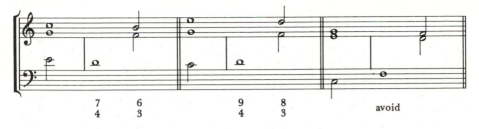

7   6   9   8
4   3   4   3   avoid

ASSIGNMENTS

Examine the passage in Ex. 8-16 and mark all examples of suspensions, noting their type, preparation, and resolution.

EXAMPLE 8-16

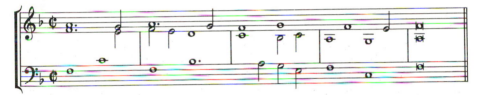

Circle and comment on the stylistic errors you note in Ex. 8-17. Take into consideration spacing, doubling, voice-leading (particularly as regards perfect intervals), and overall handling of dissonance (passing tones and suspensions).

EXAMPLE 8-17

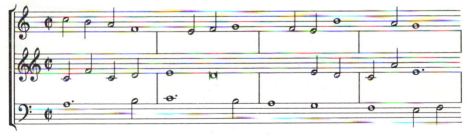

(continues on following pg.)

EXAMPLE 8-17   (*continued*)

Write a passage of nonimitative three-voice counterpoint for *cantus*, *altus*, and *tenor* with all parts beginning together. Break off the piece after about ten measures. Try to use at least one example of a 4-3, 7-6, and 2-3 suspension, in addition to various passing tones. Continue to employ white notes only; no text is necessary.

9

Cadences in Three-Voice Texture; Other White-Note Dissonance

After a survey of the cadential possibilities in three-voice compositions, the remaining instances of white-note dissonance will be discussed.

CADENCES IN THREE VOICES

During the fifteenth century, as exemplified in the so-called Burgundian school, the 7-6 suspension resolving to the octave in the *cantus* and *tenor* formed the basic structural duet for cadence formulas. The remaining third voice, or *contratenor*, was then added in various ways. From these resulting prototypes eventually evolved the cadences of the Late Renaissance. Since there is little standard terminology in the theoretical treatises of the time associated with three-voice cadences, several expressions appropriated from common-practice tonal procedures have been employed to aid in their identification.[1]

The formula shown in Ex. 9-1A, represents a typical $\frac{7\,6}{3}$ early fifteenth century cadence; note the pair of "leading tones" (E to F and B to C). The B♮ was gradually changed to a B♭, producing a diminished triad in first inversion (Ex. 9-1B). The 7-6 Phrygian cadence still retained its $\frac{6}{3}$ minor triad, although often the middle voice resolved to a major third

---

[1]These terms have been borrowed from Soderlund, *Direct Approach*, pp. 74–5.

EXAMPLE 9-1

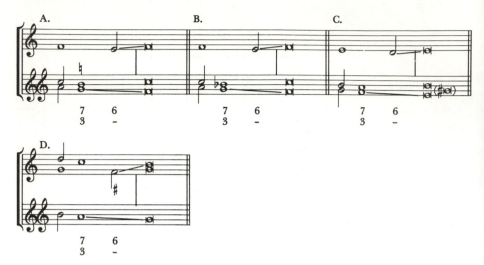

(the G♯) rather than the perfect fifth (Ex. 9-1C). If the third voice was added *above* the structural 7-6, as in Ex. 9-1D, it invariably moved to a major third to avoid the resultant parallel fifths. This formula will hereafter be referred to as a *leading-tone* cadence.

In the Burgundian cadence illustrated in Ex. 9-2A, the *contratenor* was first placed below the 7-6 suspension, and then leaped an octave upon its resolution. This was eventually modified to the form shown in Ex. 9-2B, producing a $^{5-}_{43}$ above the bass. One may also commonly find instances of Ex. 9-2C, where the 7-6 suspension has been inverted into the familiar 2-3 formula. Note that in the latter two cases all the voices resolve to an empty octave. Near the end of the sixteenth century, however, one may encounter instances of the nonsuspended upper voice moving to a major third in the final sonority (Ex. 9-2D). The basic type of 4-3 cadence becomes increasingly common during this period; for sake of reference it will be termed an *authentic* cadence.

EXAMPLE 9-2

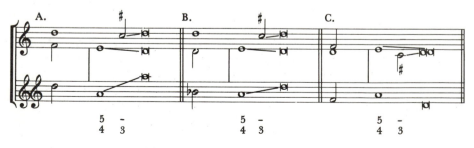

All of the above examples have been illustrated in white notes to emphasize the basic suspension technique and voice-leading. Some instances of these same cadences are shown in Ex. 9-3A through C with typical blacknote elaboration. A frequently encountered formula involves the use of a minim passing tone against an accompanying leap, which prepares the suspension (Ex. 9-3D). An occasional augmentation of an embellished suspension, as shown in Ex. 9-3E, can be found; it is restricted to final cadences only.

EXAMPLE 9-3

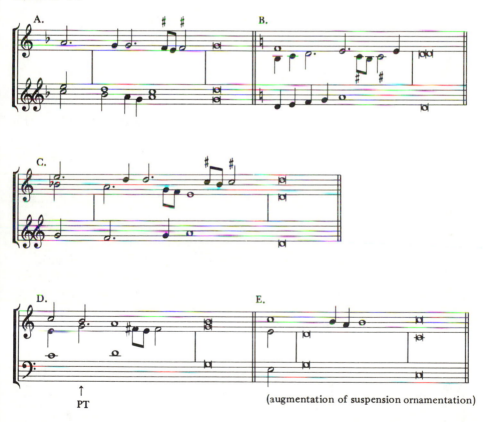

PT

(augmentation of suspension ornamentation)

The remaining cadential formula is normally encounterd at the conclusion of a composition. Its fifteenth-century prototype is shown in Ex. 9-4A. Here the *cantus-tenor* duet outlines a Phrygian cadence on A, with the *contratenor* added below. This eventually evolved into the standard form of Ex. 9-4B; note that the last sonority is always a complete triad. In terms of tonal harmony this resembles a "half cadence" in G minor; however, one must remember that the concluding chord is built on the *finalis* of the mode, so that perhaps the term *plagal* is more appropriate. Several typical elaborations of this cadence were shown in Ex. 9-4C and D. Often, plagal formulas appear as a kind of miniature codetta following the more structural 4-3 cadence. This may represent the origin of the stereotyped formula in which a movement toward the subdominant is encountered over a tonic pedal as a closing gesture; this cliché may be found well into the Classical period. One such instance is illustrated in Ex. 9-4E.

EXAMPLE 9-4

Several other types of cadential formulas may occur at the conclusions of interior phrases in a piece. Sometimes the bass of an authentic cadence will not resolve into the octave but, instead, move to some other tone, often in ascending stepwise motion, creating a type of *deceptive* formula. This is particularly useful in preserving the tonal flow of the music. Several instances are shown in Ex. 9-5.

EXAMPLE 9-5

The interrupted cadence of two-part writing still finds its counterpart in three-voices as an interior punctuation. Now, two of the voices resolve to an octave or unison, while the third part is free to initiate the next point of imitation in the following phrase. Observe, however, that the suspended voice is required to resolve. Several instances of this procedure are quoted in Ex. 9-6. The usual minim rest occurs in the *cantus* and *bassus* respectively.

EXAMPLE 9-6

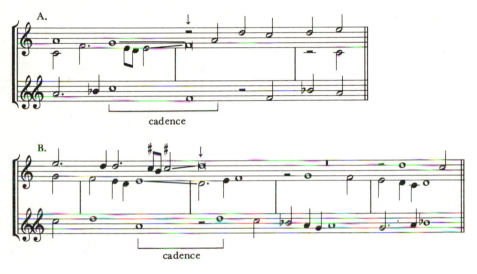

In order to preserve the seamless quality of the polyphony, a form of *overlapping* (or dovetailing) is sometimes incorporated as an interior cadence. Here the leading voice of the next point of imitation enters *before* the cadential formula is completed. This will usually involve the interrupted format discussed above. The overlap is normally not more than four minims in duration. Although this type of punctuation requires a bit more ingenuity on the part of the composer, it is particularly effective in maintaining the rhythmic flow of the music. A typical instance is shown in Ex. 9-7.

EXAMPLE 9-7

ASSIGNMENT

Complete the final cadences in three voices, using the frameworks shown in Ex. 9-8. Identify the cadence type and mode of each. Then compose an original interior cadence of either the interrupted or dovetailing variety. Start about a measure before the cadential formula and begin the first few notes of the following point of imitation in all three voices of the next phrase.

EXAMPLE 9-8

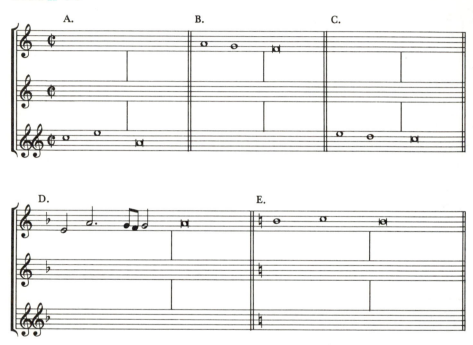

OTHER WHITE-NOTE DISSONANCE

Two other dissonant combinations involving white notes remain to be discussed: the $\frac{6}{5}$ sonority and the so-called *consonant fourth*.

The $\frac{6}{5}$ is technically not a dissonant chord, since both upper voices are intervallically consonant with the lowest part. However, because of the presence of the dissonance of a second (or seventh) between the upper parts, the fifth above the *bassus* is usually treated as if it were a suspension. As a result, the $\frac{6}{5}$ invariably falls on a strong beat (1 or 3). Upon the resolution of the suspended fifth on the next beat, the lowest voice usually moves upward by step, a kind of change of bass. The most common form of the $^6_5$ is illustrated in Ex. 9-9A. The $^6_5$ is not normally employed as part of a cadential formula, although one may find occasional examples of such treatment. Two other typical uses are quoted in Ex. 9-9B and C. Sometimes the resolution of the $^6_5$ will result in the formation of a root-position diminished triad, as in Ex. 9-9D. However, the fifth above the *bassus* in the actual $^6_5$ is almost always perfect (Ex. 9-9E). The final two examples illustrate exceptions to the normal treatment. In Ex. 9-9F, the sixth is prepared and resolved! A rather rare "free" handling occurs in Ex. 9-9G, emphasizing the consonant relation of the chordal intervals to the lowest part.

EXAMPLE 9-9

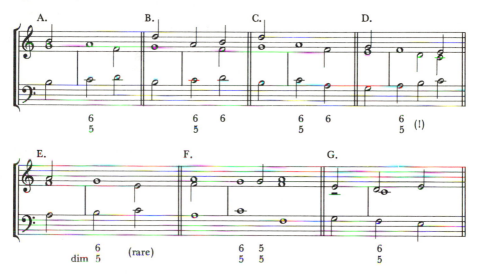

The *consonant fourth* is a device normally used to prolong the "dominant" in the *bassus* of authentic cadences. The origin of the term arises from the fact that the fourth, occurring on a weak beat above the lowest voice, serves as the preparation for the following 4-3 suspension, a function usually assigned to a strictly consonant interval. In reduction it resembles a kind of neighboring $^6_4$ over the cadential "dominant." The fourth is approached stepwise and the sustained *bassus* must be sounding *prior* to the introduction of the fourth. The normal form of this device is shown in Ex. 9-10A. Note the voice-crossing in Ex. 9-10D, the first C in the *cantus* is a passing tone. In Ex. 9-10C the $^6_4$ results from the resolution of a $^7_3$ suspension; this is a particularly favorite device of the English school. Finally, the $^6_5$ and consonant fourth are frequently combined; the use of the *portamento* is common in this context (Ex. 9-10D).

EXAMPLE 9-10

ASSIGNMENTS

Using the passage in Ex. 9-11, circle any incorrect stylistic procedures and comment upon them.

EXAMPLE 9-11

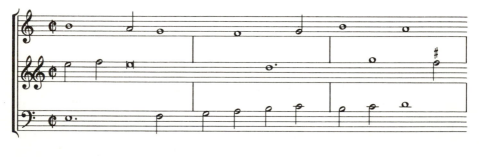

Write an example of nonimitative three-voice polyphony of about ten measures in duration. Choose an appropriate cadence for your mode, and try to incorporate at least one example of a $^6_5$ and consonant fourth, in addition to the usual white-note passing tones and suspensions. No text is necessary.

10

Black Notes in Three-Voice Texture; Imitation and Reentries

For the most part, those procedures observed in two-voice writing that involve the use of black notes continue to be followed in three-part texture. The following additional comments may be noted.

Essential harmonic leaps may occur in other parts against semiminim passing tones, either unaccented or accented. In Ex. 10-1A the *cantus* leaps against the accented passing tone in the *altus*, which forms part of a filled-in *cambiata*. Observe the semiminim leap in the altus against the upper passing tone in Ex. 10-1B. Remember that such leaps must still be consonant with *both* voices, as is the procedure with such white-note situations. Ex. 10-1C illustrates an unaccented passing tone placed against the second note of a *cambiata* figure in the *altus*. As the result of the interaction between simultaneous nonharmonic tones, occasional dissonant parallels occur. In Ex. 10-1D a lower neighbor is combined with a consonant *portamento* to create parallel seconds. In the same manner, a lower neighbor may occur with an accented passing tone, producing parallel sevenths, as in Ex. 10-1E. Finally, the use of an accented passing tone and its subsequent resolution may be incorporated in consecutive 4-3 suspensions to avoid parallel perfect fifths in the lower voices (Ex. 10-1F).

Particular attention must be paid to the simultaneous use of a dotted minim and its following semiminim against another minim. Study the various instances quoted in Ex. 10-2, particularly noting Ex. 10-2D, which produces an incorrect suspension on the second beat.

EXAMPLE 10-1

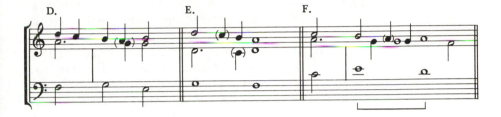

EXAMPLE 10-2

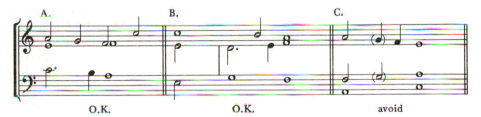

O.K.   O.K.   avoid

avoid

ASSIGNMENT

Write a passage for three adjacent voices of about eight measures in duration, employing various black-note figures in both consonant and dissonant settings. No text is necessary.

IMITATION AND REENTRY
IN THREE-VOICE TEXTURE

Three-voice imitation almost always involves the use of some fifth-relation between a pair of the voices, either a perfect fifth or fourth up or down. This principle not only applies to the opening point of imitation but to those within interior phrases as well. In the Dorian mode, for instance, the initial pitches of the beginning point of imitation would usually be D-A-D, A-D-A, D-D-A, or A-A-D. The principle of *fuga* remains in effect, producing what might be termed "real answers" at the perfect fifth or fourth. Once the imitating voices have entered, the texture will normally break into free counterpoint.

As regards the temporal distance between the consecutive imitating voices, a variety of situations may result. Asymmetrical relations are, perhaps, more commonly encountered than symmetrical; here the distance between the second pair of entries is temporally varied from that of the initial pair. The first two voices are almost never more than four semibreves apart. The order of entry of the various voices employed (for instance, *cantus, altus, tenor*) shows no clear-cut tendency. Several examples of initial points of imitation are quoted from the literature of the period below. In Ex. 10-3 the Phrygian mode is employed, hence the use of pitch classes E-A-A. Since the temporal distance between the entries is symmetrical (four semibreves) double counterpoint at the twelfth is used so that the relationships between the first fifth-imitation may later be preserved at the octave; compare the *tenor* and *bassus* in measures 3-4 with those of the *altus* and *bassus* in measures 5-6. The opening E-F (Mi-Fa) necessitates the use of a B♭ in the entry on A.

EXAMPLE 10-3

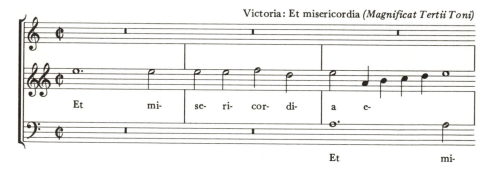

Victoria: Et misericordia *(Magnificat Tertii Toni)*

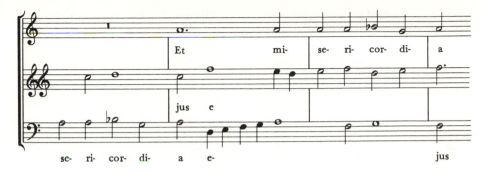

Ex. 10-4 makes use of the transposed Mixolydian mode with pitch classes C-G-C. Here the temporal entries are asymmetrical with distances of one and four semibreves respectively. The opening imitation is almost stretto-like in its effect.

EXAMPLE 10-4

Palestrina: Sanctus (*Missa de Beata Virgine*)

Asymmetrical temporal distances are also encountered in Ex. 10-5 with three and four semibreves employed. The customary pitch classes of the transposed Dorian may be noted (D-G-G). The occurrence of the tonal answers in the last pair of entries is rather unusual; apparently the composer was intent on strongly establishing the quality of a G minor triad. It may be observed that most tonal answers involve the modification of a perfect fifth or fourth. This procedure may represent the origin of tonal answers involving tonic and dominant in baroque fugal technique.

EXAMPLE 10-5

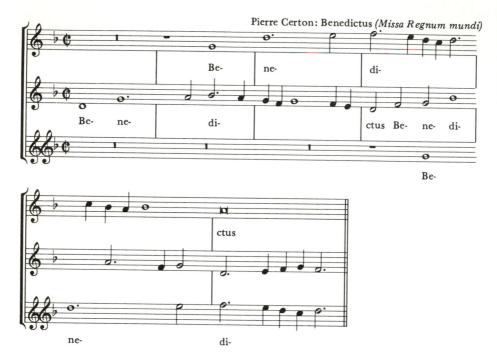

Pierre Certon: Benedictus *(Missa Regnum mundi)*

Those principles observed in initial points of imitation hold true, for the most part, in instances of interior points of imitation following internal cadences. The thematic subjects of interior phrases appear to take on a motivic character and the temporal distances between entries are kept to a minimum. As mentioned in the discussion of two-voice polyphony, themes beginning on weak beats are common. Fifth-relationships between pitch classes of the imitating voices are still retained. The initial tones are generally related to important structural notes of the mode in addition to their attendant fifth-relations. Thus, in the Dorian mode, interior points of imitation beginning on F-C or A-E—in addition to D-A—would be frequent. The diagram in Fig. 10-1 summarizes the various points of imitation in a short composition, as regards their tonal and temporal characteristics. The major cadential points are also included.

FIGURE 10-1 Thematic Entries in Certon: Benedictus (*Missa Regnum mundi*)

Each subject entry denoted by ×××× (Benedictus), ○○○○ (qui venit), and ﹏﹏ (in nomine Domini); free counterpoint by a straight line.

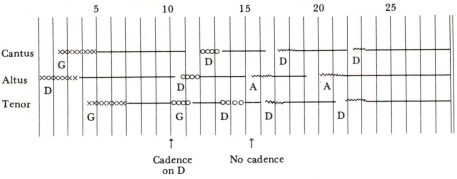

Reentries of the original thematic subject within the phrase show a marked inclination on the part of composers to retain the initial pitch classes found in the opening fifth-relation. While this is by no means totally consistent, it does appear to represent a strong stylistic feature on the continent. Tonal adjustments and slight rhythmic alterations are not uncommon in reentries. The *in nomine Domini* section of the Benedictus in Ex. 10-6 provides an opportunity to observe this mannerism. Study this passage carefully as regards the various reentries; it may be observed that the use of B as an initial imitating tone is rather uncommon.

EXAMPLE 10-6

Lassus: *Laudabo nomen Dei* (motet)

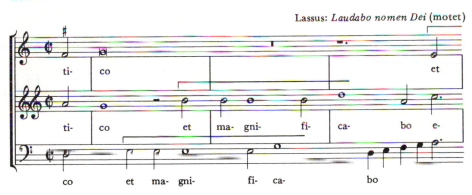

(continues on following pg.)

EXAMPLE 10-6   *(continued)*

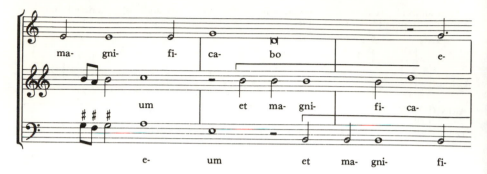

ASSIGNMENTS

Write two opening points of imitation for three voices on the text below. Employ different voice entrances, temporal distances, and intervallic relations between the parts. Incorporate real answers in accord with *fuga* principles.

Ký- ri- é   e-   lé-   i-   són[1]

(Lord   have mercy)

Reproduced in Ex. 10-7 is a short Benedictus of Lassus, in which only the basic imitative entries or reentries have been included. Fill in the remaining voices with appropriate counterpoint and text-setting. Note the interior point of imitation on the words *in nomine* in regard to subsequent reentries of the *in nomine* theme.

Bé- ne dí- ctus   qui vén it,   in nó- mi-   ne   Dó- mi- ni.

(Blessed is he   who   comes   in   the name   of the Lord)

EXAMPLE 10-7

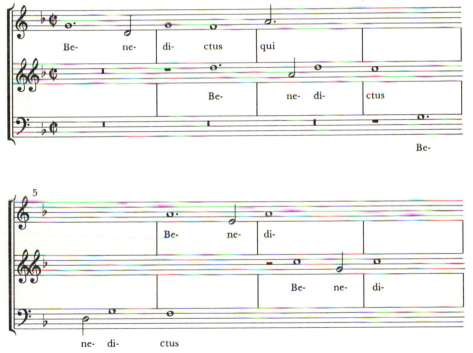

Lassus: Benedictus *(Missa pro defunctis)*

(continues on following pg.)

---

[1]These two words may be set in several different ways: Ky-ri-e or Ky-rie, and e-le-i-son or e-lei-son.

EXAMPLE 10-7   (*continued*)

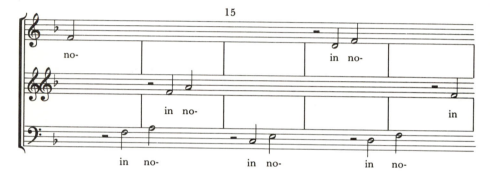

11

Paraphrase Technique; Further Studies in Canon

In addition to a discussion of paraphrase technique, this chapter will include an exploration of the problems encountered in three-voice canonic writing.

PARAPHRASE TECHNIQUE

Since the inception of counterpoint with *organum*, the practice of basing polyphonic pieces on preexistent musical material has remained one of its most common procedures. The Late Renaissance is no exception in this regard. As concerns musical settings of the Ordinary of the Mass, one may note that out of roughly one hundred examples by Palestrina, less than five are "free compositions," the remainder finding their origins in preexistent sources. At least three distinct means of employing preexistent material can be found. The use of *cantus firmus* and *parody* techniques will be discussed in detail in chapters 14 and 17, respectively. We will limit ourselves for the present to the remaining procedure, that of *paraphrase*. During its initial development in the Early Renaissance, it involves the elaborated quotation of a given chant in only one of the voices. In its later stages, the plainsong is given to the other voices in the points of imitation. By the sixteenth century, the pitch series of each separate phrase of the chant forms the tonal material for the themes of the successive points of imitation in a polyphonic piece.[1] The complete chant phrase is quoted in its entirety in at least *one* of the voices, and it may even be incorporated in *all* the parts. The derivation of the subsequent themes from the original plainsong is always fairly obvious. However, some license was allowed. One may observe instances of *ellipsis* (omission of one or more notes), *interpolation* of a note, *ornamentation,* and even *extension.* In addition, transposition, usually at some fifth-relation, is not uncommon. In the case of the mass, new text is substituted for that of the original chant.

The basic compositional problem for the student employing this technique is the arrangement of the original pitch series of the plainsong in such a rhythmic fashion that, in a point of imitation, the opening motive will overlap in imitation while still employing the fifth-relationships normally encountered in three voices. The first five notes of a hypothetical chant are given in Ex. 11-1. Study the two opening points of imitation based on this phrase in Ex. 11-2 and 11-3; the chant is bracketed in each voice. The examples are in the Ionian and Lydian modes, respectively.

EXAMPLE 11-1

Ca-   tho-   li-   cam

EXAMPLE 11-2

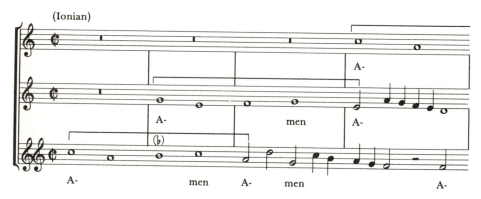

[1]For an illuminating article on Palestrina's use of this device the reader is referred to Robert L. Marshall, "The Paraphrase Technique of Palestrina in His Masses Based on Hymns," *Journal of the American Musicological Society,* 16/3 (1963), pp. 347–72.

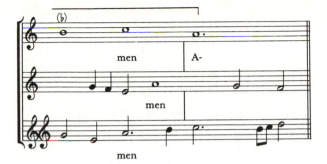

EXAMPLE 11-3

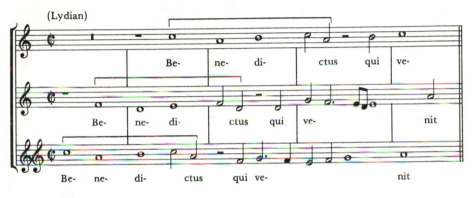

ASSIGNMENTS

As a model of paraphrase technique in an entire movement, a short poly-phonic setting by Palestrina based on the hymn *Ad preces nostras* is quoted in Ex. 11-5. The original plainsong, with each pitch numbered, is given in Ex. 11-4.[2] Note that one of the voices in each point of imitation will present the chant phrase in longer note values; these voice parts are indicated below each phrase of the chant in Ex. 11-4. Trace the manner in which the successive phrases of the chant are incorporated into the various points of imitation, and as reentries in the successive sections of the piece, by using the numbers of the chant pitches. Change of text will serve as a clue in dividing the various phrases. The mode is Lydian, although the final cadence is on A, not an infrequent occurrence in this mode. Can you find any examples of dovetailing cadences?

---

[2]This numbering system has been adopted from the excellent article on paraphrase procedure by Irving Godt, "Renaissance Paraphrase Technique: A Descriptive Tool," *Music Theory Spectrum*, 2 (1980), pp. 110–18.

EXAMPLE 11-4

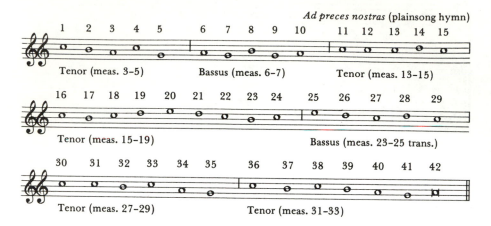

Ad preces nostras (plainsong hymn)

Tenor (meas. 3–5)   Bassus (meas. 6–7)   Tenor (meas. 13–15)

Tenor (meas. 15–19)   Bassus (meas. 23–25 trans.)

Tenor (meas. 27–29)   Tenor (meas. 31–33)

EXAMPLE 11-5

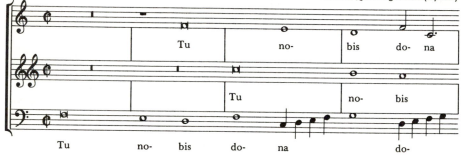

Palestrina: *In Dominicis Quadragesima* (hymn)

Tu   no-   bis   do-   na

Tu   no-   bis

Tu   no-   bis   do-   na   do-

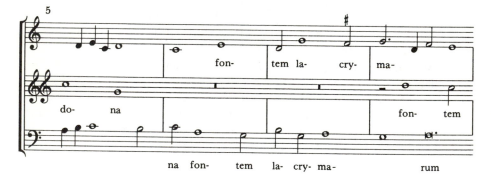

fon-   tem la-   cry-   ma-

do-   na   fon-   tem

na fon-   tem   la-   cry- ma-   rum

(continues on following pg.)

EXAMPLE 11-5 (*continued*)

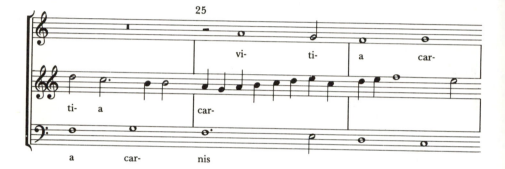

Using the three extracted phrases from the plainsong *Pange lingua*,[3] write a three-voice composition in paraphrase technique using the following text:

Ág-	nus	Dé-	i,	qui	tól-	lis	pec-	cá-	ta	mún-	di,
(Lamb		of God,		who	takes	away		the sins		of the world,	

mí-	se-	ré-	re	nó-	bis.
have	mercy			on us.)	

The original chant phrases and their respective text are given in Ex. 11-6.

As the mode is Phrygian, the most likely pitch classes for the opening point of imitation would be E and A, although E and B are possible. One student's realization of the first phrase is illustrated in Ex. 11-7. In this case each voice continues the chant phrase to its conclusion. This is not absolutely necessary in every case, although one would normally expect at least one of the parts to function in this manner.

Plot the interior cadences of the piece in relation to the mode, making

---

[3]For an analysis of the Kyrie from Josquin's *Missa Pange lingua*, based on this chant, see Godt, "Renaissance Paraphrase Technique," pp. 111–15.

EXAMPLE 11-6

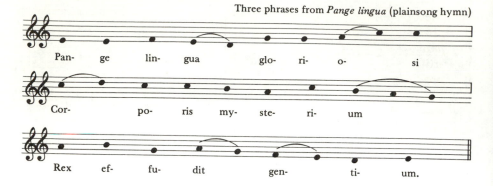

Three phrases from *Pange lingua* (plainsong hymn)

Pan- ge lin- gua glo- ri- o- si

Cor- po- ris my- ste- ri- um

Rex ef- fu- dit gen- ti- um.

EXAMPLE 11-7

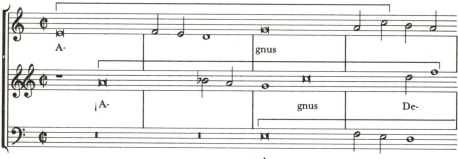

A- gnus

A- gnus De-

A-

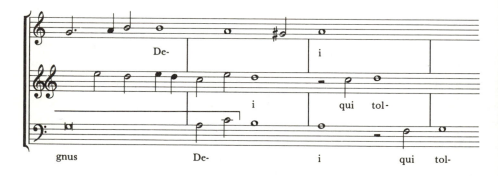

De- i

i qui tol-

gnus De- i qui tol-

sure that the new pitch classes for each succeeding point of imitation, based in turn on the chant, "plug in" tonally to the preceding interior cadence. For example, the first cadence might center on C, which would allow the next phrase to occur on the fifth-relation of C and G. It is possible to work the last notes of the final chant phrase into a three-voice Phrygian cadence to end the piece. Try to include at least one reentry of the subject in the last two phrases.

THREE-VOICE CANONS (3 IN 1)

As noted previously in chapter 6 the use of canonic technique, particularly in textures involving three or more voices, had declined in this period, as compared with its more frequent employment in the fifteenth century. Nevertheless, composers of the Late Renaissance occasionally returned to this procedure as a means of demonstrating their technical ability within a strict, confined discipline.[4] One may sometimes encounter "canonic" masses—entire works written largely in this style (so-called *missa ad fugam*).

The method of writing a two-voice canon is relatively simple, in that the *consequente* voice strictly imitates the *guida* voice at some given perfect interval (*fuga legate*). The problems involved with the composition of a three-voice canon, however, increase almost geometrically. The possible ways of laying out the opening point of imitation will be discussed first. Perhaps the simplest method is to commence with the uppermost part and then imitate the lower voices in succession at the *same* intervallic relation (usually a perfect fifth or fourth below) and at the *same* temporal distance, creating a kind of symmetrical point of imitation. The opening measures of a canon employing this approach are illustrated in Ex. 11-8; the interval imitation is at the subdiatesseron and the time distance is two semibreves. Obviously, the technique may also be reversed, beginning with the lowest voice first. With symmetrical three-voice canons the *fuga* concept employed in the *consequente* voices is usually dropped. Thus with a subject answered by successive descending fourths, CDEF = GABC = DEF♮ G, not DEF♯ G. In this regard consult the opening of Ex. 8-11. In situations similar to those shown in Ex. 11-8, the intervallic relations between the upper pair of voices are successively transferred to the lower two parts. One must therefore be on guard for the occurrences of perfect fourths, as they cannot appear as consonant intervals between the lower voices. In particular, one

EXAMPLE 11-8

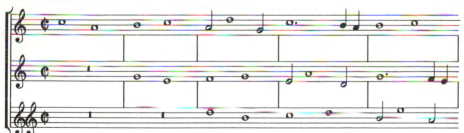

(continues on following pg.)

[4]Additional information on canon may be found in Alfred Mann and J. Kenneth Wilson, "Canon 1.," *The New Groves Dictionary* Vol. 3, pp. 689–90.

Also see Willi Apel, "Imitation Canons on L'homme armé," *Speculum*, 25 (1950), p. 367.

EXAMPLE 11-8   *(continued)*

must watch for $^6_3$ sonorities containing fourths (consult Ex. 11-9A in this regard). Also, one must be careful about using thematic ideas containing excessive numbers of melodic leaps of fourths or fifths, as tritone problems can result with imitating voices later on (as shown in Ex. 11-9B).

EXAMPLE 11-9

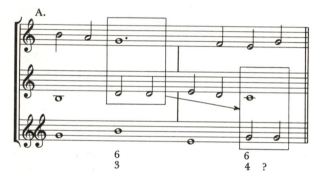

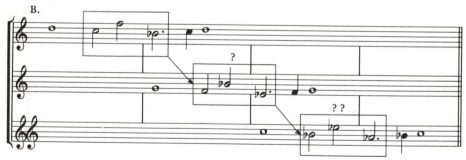

Ex. 11-10 utilizes symmetrical temporal distances of four semibreves between the parts but with the use of a single fifth-relation (C-F-F) typical of conventional three-voice points of imitation. Obviously, the intervallic relations between the initial two voices, a fifth apart, will not hold constant with the octave imitation of the latter two. In cases of this nature, the employment of some type of double counterpoint may prove useful. Notice that double counterpoint at the twelfth has been employed; the *bassus* voice is subsequently transposed up an octave and the *tenor* down a perfect fifth in measures 5-6 (8 + 5 = 13).

EXAMPLE 11-10

Opening points of canonic imitation employing *both* asymmetrical intervallic and temporal relations create extreme problems as regards the continuation of the strict imitation. In Ex. 11-11 the fifth-relation (C-G-C) is used with distances of two and four semibreves respectively. Note that the

EXAMPLE 11-11

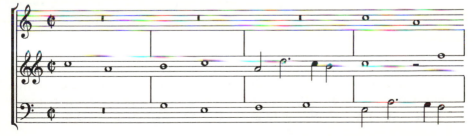

(continues on following pg.)

EXAMPLE 11-11   *(continued)*

counterpoint in the third measure of the *tenor* must now also be able to "work" with the upper voice when it is transferred to the *bassus* in the fourth measure. Are there other similar situations?

Another problem is the setting up of cadential formulas within the strict, canonic texture, two of the voices of the cadence having already appeared earlier, although at a different pitch level. Study the final cadence of the symmetrical canon shown in Ex. 11-12. In this leading-tone cadence the A-G of the *bassus* has been anticipated in the previous measures (G-F → D-C → A-G). In addition, the *altus* suspension has been set up in the *cantus* a measure before (C-B-C → G-F♯-G).

EXAMPLE 11-12

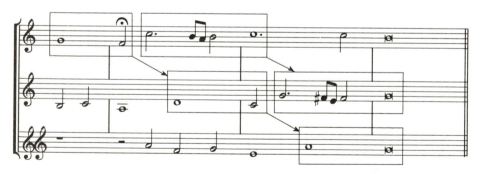

The same situation, of course, occurs in interior cadences as well. It is small wonder that three-voice canons are not always the best source for the study of interior cadential punctuation. Ex. 11-13 illustrates an interrupted interior authentic cadence; note again the anticipatory technique.

EXAMPLE 11-13

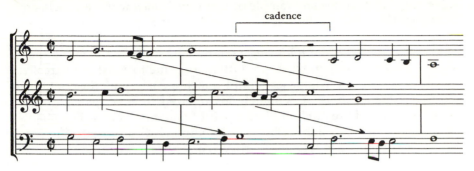

ASSIGNMENTS

Make a careful analysis of the three-voice canonic "Benedictus" from Palestrina's *Missa ad fugam* in Ex. 12-5, noting the various techniques discussed above.[5]

Ex. 11-14 quotes the leading or *guida cantus* voice of the famous *Non nobis Domine*, sometimes attributed to William Byrd.[6] Realize the complete canon for three voices. The temporal distances are denoted by the *presa* signs (furnished here by the author); however, the student must determine

EXAMPLE 11-14

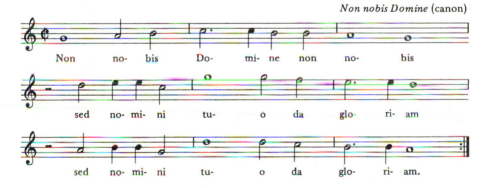

Non nobis Domine (canon)

[5]Four other canonic movements from this mass are quoted in Soderlund and Scott, *Examples of Gregorian Chant*, a three-voice Pleni sunt caeli (pp. 104–5), a four voice Kyrie and Sanctus (p. 214–16), and a very interesting five-voice Agnus Dei (pp. 218–19), which will repay careful analysis.

[6]Byrd worked out a number of canonic realizations for this melody, including examples in both two and three voices.

the intervallic relations between the imitating voices. The use of repeat signs suggests that it is an example of a *perpetual canon* without conclusion. Do you note any stylistic deviations in both the given *guida* and your realization?

As a preface to the following assignment, study the opening measures of the *guida* voice in Ex. 11-15. Often, as a clue to assist in the realization of a canon, the composer would attach some cryptic inscription or phrase, resulting in what is sometimes referred to as a *"puzzle canon."*[7] Here the twofold "rejoice" implies a pair of imitating voices. The chapter and verse numbers might refer to the temporal distance (at four semibreves) and intervallic relation (each voice a perfect fourth lower).

EXAMPLE 11-15

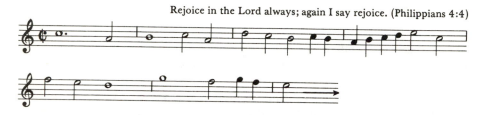

Rejoice in the Lord always; again I say rejoice. (Philippians 4:4)

The complete realization is given in Ex. 11-16.

EXAMPLE 11-16

---

[7]Two examples of puzzle canons appear in Ex. 12-6.

Compose an original three-part "puzzle canon" without text. After you have completed your full score, write out only the *guida* voice and include some accompanying phrase or phrases that contain hidden clues as to the intervallic and temporal distances at which the imitating voices enter. Be sure to include a *coronata* sign (⌒) to denote the last imitated note in the leader voice. Then, exchange papers with your fellow students to see if the proper realizations can be arrived at.

12

Examples of Three-Voice Compositions for Analysis

A variety of three-voice genre are illustrated here, including examples of additive procedure, paraphrase technique, and three instances of canonic treatment.

EXAMPLE 12-1: Josquin: *Ave verum Pars II* (motet - 1503).

Each *pars* of this interesting little miniature is divided into two sections; the first of each consists of a two-voice setting for a pair of upper voices; the music of the duet (with different text) is then repeated *exactly* with a lower part added to complete the three-voice polyphony. Only the final section of *Pars II* is quoted here. Examine the upper parts first as an example of a self-contained duet, and then consider the additional voice in regard to the principles of three-part writing. Note the frequent use of *cambiata* and the curious section from measures 19-21 employing only dotted minims and semiminims.

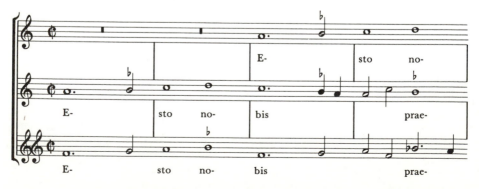

(continues on following pg.)

EXAMPLE 12-1   *(continued)*

Es- to no- bis prae- gu- sta- tum mor- tis in ex- a- min- ne.
(Be   to us   a foretaste   death's in   test)

EXAMPLE 12-2:   Lassus: *Ego sum pauper Pars I* (motet - 1577).

The text for this example comes from Psalms 68:30; *Pars II* is based on the following verse. The piece is divided into three well-defined sections. Although the opening point of imitation is symmetrical with all three entries on A, subsequent reentries of the subject feature a variety of different tones (F, A, G, and C). Notice the *stretto* in measures 10-11. The final section, beginning in measure 23 with the overlapping cadence, comprises a fascinating study in white-note suspension technique. In what way is this setting related to the text?

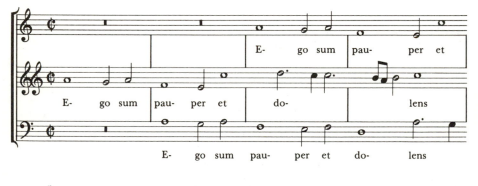

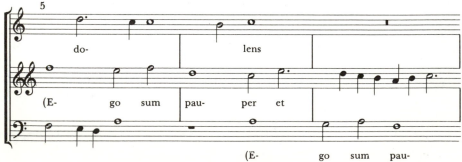

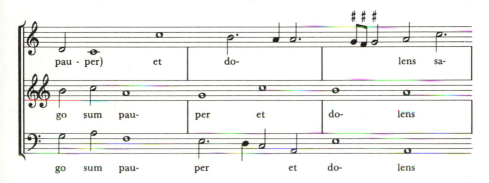

(continues on following pg.)

EXAMPLE 12-2   *(continued)*

E- go sum pau- er et do- lens, sa- lus tu- a De- us si- sce- pit me.
(I　am　poor　and distressed, salvation your,　God,　accepted　me.)

EXAMPLE 12-3:　Palestrina: Benedictus from his *Missa de feria* (1570).

The next three examples are settings of the Benedictus by Palestrina. Although the Sanctus of this abbreviated mass incorporates chant paraphrase, the procedure is not employed in the Benedictus. This piece is particularly rich in various dissonant devices (suspension, $^6_5$, consonant fourth, *cambiata*, etc.). Analyze it thoroughly in this respect.

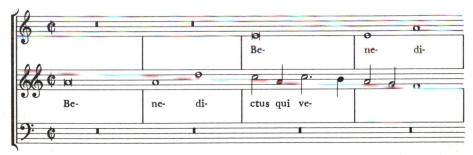

(continues on following pg.)

EXAMPLE 12-3 *(continued)*

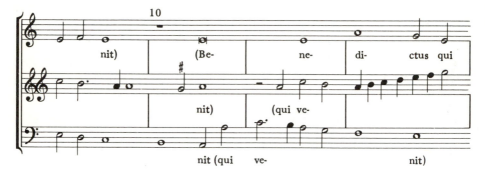

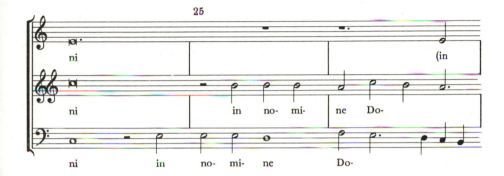

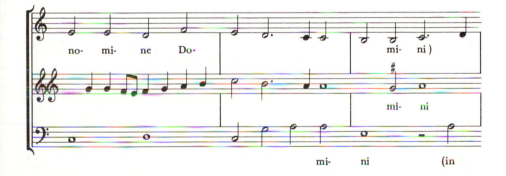

(continues on following pg.)

EXAMPLE 12-3   *(continued)*

Benedictus   qui venit in nomine   Domini.
(Blessed is he who comes in the name of the Lord.)

EXAMPLE 12-4:   Palestrina: Benedictus from his *Missa Aeterna Christi munera* (1590).

A classic example of paraphrase technique, this movement is based on two phrases of the chant quoted below. Trace the relationships of the themes to the plainsong melody, employing the numbering system discussed previously. Some degree of liberty has been taken with the last phrase. Locate any illustrations of overlapping cadences in the *in nomine* section. Are there any instances of *stretto* in this work?

(continues on following pg.)

EXAMPLE 12-4   *(continued)*

EXAMPLE 12-5: Palestrina: Benedictus from his *Missa ad fugam* (1567).

An example of three-voice canonic writing, entitled *Trinitas in unitate*, this movement is typical of the strict imitative technique found throughout this mass. It is a model of successive symmetrical entrances, each voice being a perfect fifth lower, at the distance of four semibreves. Observe the manner in which Palestrina sets up his interior and final cadential points (measures 6-7, 8-9, and 19-20), noting the means by which he avoids parallels in the first instance.

(continues on following pg.)

EXAMPLE 12-5   (*continued*)

EXAMPLE 12-6:   Anonymous Puzzle Canon from *Henry VIII's Manuscript* (c. 1515?); William Byrd: *Puzzle Canon* (c. 1570?).

Two realizations of puzzle canons from the English school follow. The inscription from the first piece reads as follows: Thys songe is iij parts in one and eche part begynnyth under the other; the secund parte rests iij and begynnyth is alamire underneth; the iij^d part rest v and begynnyth in gesolreut beneth. Byrd's ingenious little exercise employs a chant *cantus firmus* (based on a *miserere*). Above the lower voice he adds the phrase *Two parts in one*. In what way are the two *bassus* parts canonic? (Hint: see measure 7.) What problems are encountered in the writing of a work like this? There is some freedom in the rhythmic handling of the lower voices, although this is not unusual in instrumental media.

Anonymous

(continues on following pg.)

EXAMPLE 12-6   *(continued)*

Byrd

13

General Considerations
of Four-Voice Texture;
Familiar Style

Four- and five-part textures may be considered the norm in the sacred music of the Late Renaissance. Some comments concerning the general handling of four voices will be presented in this chapter. In addition, the question of homorhythmic text setting as exemplified in familiar style will be discussed.

BASIC CHARACTERISTICS
OF FOUR-VOICE TEXTURE

The typical choral layout is for *cantus, altus, tenor,* and *bassus.* As noted in chapter 1, either the higher (*chiarette*) or lower (*chiari naturali*) clef system may be employed, varying the range of the voices by about a third. One may also on occasion find exceptional arrangements, such as *cantus, cantus, altus,* and *tenor* or even two *tenor* and two *bassus* voice lines.

There appears to be no overriding tendency to double a particular triadic member (root, third, or fifth); sonorities featuring doubled fifths or thirds are found about as commonly as doubled roots in polyphonic texture. Although the composers strove to maintain as complete triadic sonorities as possible, instances of momentary tripled notes are by no means unusual. However, the doubling of any raising *musica ficta* is avoided; the doubling of B♭ in its root position may be occasionally noted.

In addition, it is difficult to observe any basic consistency as regards the spacing of chords in typical polyphonic passages. Various arrangements of "close and open" (less or more than an octave between the *cantus* and *tenor*) are encountered. Large intervallic distances between consecutive upper parts are not ordinarily featured for long periods of time, although brief instances of voice crossing are permissible. Study Ex. 13-1 in light of the above discussion.

EXAMPLE 13-1

de La Rue: *O Salutaris hostia*

Parallel perfect intervals are still forbidden. Also, one must be on guard against any instances of "contrary" octaves or fifths (Ex. 13-2). One may encounter instances of similar (or direct) octaves. Otherwise, the rules regulating the approach and departure of perfect intervals are similar to those noted in three-voice texture; in this regard review chapter 8.

EXAMPLE 13-2

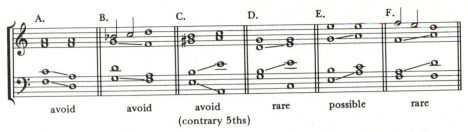

The most common cadential formulas may be thought of as basic expansions of those found in three-voice writing. The 4-3 authentic cadence tends to become more frequent as the number of parts increases. In the suspension the additional fourth voice usually doubles the bassus, as in Ex. 13-3A through D. Note that the sixth or third produced by the suspension resolution continues to move to the octave or unison respectively, thereby retaining the two-voice *clausula vera* as a basic structural duet (Ex. 13-3A through C). The *imperfetta* cadence involving a sixth to sixth may occasionally be observed, although it is not common (Ex. 13-3D). The voice-leading will normally produce an octave and a perfect fifth or major third on the last chord; it must be stressed that only major thirds are permitted in final cadence chords (Ex. 13-3A through C).

The cadential passing tone illustrated in Ex. 13-3E is very rare in the continental style, although it may be observed in the English school. On the other hand, the use of a *cambiata* figure in an inner voice is common (Ex. 13-3F).

EXAMPLE 13-3

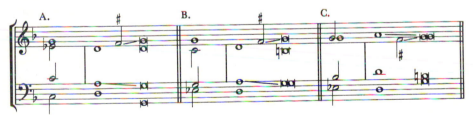

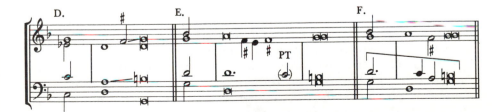

Two instances of the 7-6 leading-tone cadence type are shown in Ex. 13-4 A and B; the final chord will be a complete triad. Note the omnipresent sixth to octave resolution. In the Phrygian mode, a kind of final "root position" cadence can sometimes be encountered (Ex. 13-4C); it is not typical of the other modes.

EXAMPLE 13-4

The expansion of the plagal cadence will result in both triads being complete (Ex. 13-5A and B). Several instances of elaborated plagal formulas are illustrated in Ex. 13-5 C through D.

EXAMPLE 13-5

Palestrina: Kyrie (*Missa brevis*)

Ex. 13-6 illustrates the most common instances of suspension technique in four-voice writing. In $\frac{5}{4}$, $\frac{6}{4}$, $\frac{7}{3}$, and bass suspensions, one of the voices is frequently doubled at the octave (see Ex. 13-6A through D). However, the existence of three different pitch classes occurring above the bass at the point of suspension may occasionally be noted, particularly with the 9-8 (Ex. 13-6E). The last three instances of this procedure (Ex. 13-6F through H) suggest the origin of certain "seventh chord" suspension preparations found later in the baroque period: Ex. 13-6F = root position, Ex. 13-6G = third inversion, and Ex. 13-6H = first inversion.

EXAMPLE 13-6

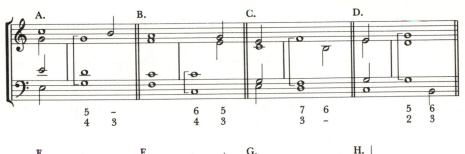

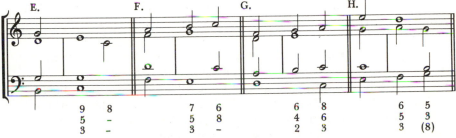

There is no perceptible difference in the general handling of black notes for four and three voices. The percentage of black-note usage is considerably less than in two- and even three-part texture.

As a general rule, when the number of parts increases, the harmonic rhythm tends to slow down correspondingly. One may tentatively state that the norm for four-voice writing is chord change by the semibreve. Excessive harmonic movement by the minim should be avoided, as the overall effect is somewhat "rushed" and the possibility of minim passing tones is eliminated.

Once all of the voices have entered following an initial point of imitation, strict four-part texture is not maintained for long periods of time. Indeed, one of the opening voices may have already dropped out by the time the last part enters. Voices are continually resting and reentering during the course of the movement. One might even state as a general norm that the usual number of voices at a given point in the interior of a piece is that of three-part writing. The texture tends to "thicken" near structural cadences. These points may be illustrated in Fig. 13-1, which shows the fluctuation of the number of voices in a typical movement.

ASSIGNMENT

Write a passage of *consistent* four-voice nonimitative texture for *cantus, altus, tenor,* and *bassus.* It should be eight to ten measures in duration. In addition to a suitable cadence, strive to include some examples of suspensions as well as various types of black-note figuration. No text is necessary.

FIGURE 13-1   Textural Variance in Palestrina: Christe (*Missa de feria*)

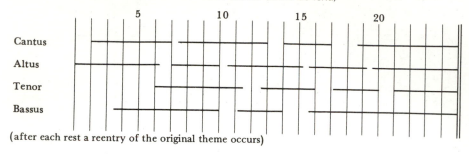

(after each rest a reentry of the original theme occurs)

FAMILIAR STYLE

Throughout the history of counterpoint, sections of works or even entire pieces have been set in a basically syllabic manner, resulting in a predominately chordal or homorhythmic style. Witness the *conductus* of the medievel period. The term used to describe this technique in the Late Renaissance is *stile familiare* (or familiar style). Its most frequent use may be found in hymn settings, responses, certain motets, and in various sections of the Gloria or Credo as well as the Hosanna of the Mass. Obviously, the main reason for employing this declamatory procedure is to cover a large amount of text within a short length of time.

Some general characteristics of familiar style in four voices are listed below. These same features will hold true for a greater number of parts as well. The upper three voices are normally in close structure (less than an octave between *cantus* and *tenor*). The consonant sonorities show a strong tendency toward root position ($\frac{5}{3}$), with first inversion ($\frac{6}{3}$) being somewhat of an exception. The *bassus* note (or root of the triad) is usually doubled; as stated previously, doubling of any raised *musica ficta* is avoided. Nonharmonic motion is kept to an absolute minimum, although suspensions (such as $\frac{5}{4}\frac{}{3}$) are still found at cadential points. As one might suspect in a declamatory style, repeated chords are common. Metric shifts in the underlying microrhythm can still be observed. Study the short excerpt in Ex. 13-7 in light of the preceding discussion; the implied metric changes have been indicated.

EXAMPLE 13-7

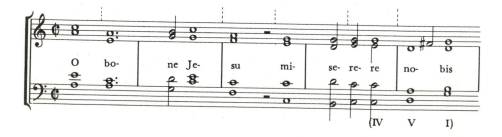

qui- a tu   cre-   a- sti   nos   tu   re- de- mi-   sti   nos.

(IV   V   I)

The emphasis away from polyphonic procedures results in a greater attention given the purely harmonic aspect of such passages. In our previous analysis of the music of this period, raised *musica ficta* were usually confined to cadence points, either as a leading tone or as the raised third of the final sonority. However, in familiar style one sometimes notes the employment of *musica ficta* for more "coloristic" or harmonic purposes, thereby altering the natural pitch class chord types (D F A becoming D F♯ A or G B D becoming G B♭ D). The normal accidentals of C♯, F♯, G♯, and B♭ (in the untransposed mode) are still employed; the use of more exotic *musica ficta* (D♯, A♯, A♭, etc.) is actually more typical of the secular music near the end of the century and should be avoided at present.[1] Two examples of this coloristic mannerism may be noted in the short passage from Palestrina's *Missa Jesu nostra redemptio* (Ex. 13-8).[2] In measures 3 - 6 (see brackets) a succession of triads by falling fifth-relation occurs. Observe that appropriate *musica ficta* has been applied to render each chord a major sonority, producing a sequence not unlike a progression of "secondary dominants." In measure 10, the A major triad acts as the cadence for the preceding phrase. The following phrase now commences on an A minor sonority, creating a cross relation between the *altus* and *cantus* (C♯ - C♮). This change of mode involving the same chord is commonly encountered between phrases, particularly in the English school.

EXAMPLE 13-8

Palestrina: Credo (*Missa Jesu nostra redemptio*)

Et   in-   car-   na- tus   est   de   Spi-

(continues on following pg.)

[1] This topic will be discussed in chapter 22.

[2] This section of the Credo beginning with the words *Et incarnatus est* is customarily set in homorhythmic style using longer note values.

EXAMPLE 13-8   *(continued)*

ri- tu San- cto ex Ma- ri- a Vir- gi-

ne Et ho- mo fa- ctus est.

The most frequent root movement between chords is by perfect fifth and major second, either descending or ascending. Some motion by falling thirds may be observed, while tritone relations are almost nonexistent. The use of minor-second movement is somewhat limited; two common instances are shown in Ex. 13-9.

EXAMPLE 13-9

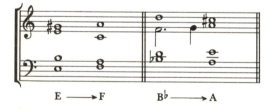

E ⟶ F   B♭ ⟶ A

One might wish to think of the basic harmonic motion as progressing either toward the sharp (or brighter) side through *ascending* fifths (major triads of C-G-D-A-E) or toward the flat (or darker) side by *descending* fifths (major triads of G-C-F-B♭). Fig. 13-2 illustrations this coloristic gamut.

The movement of major triads by major second will tend to accelerate this motion (D-C-B♭). The ascending major second relation is also useful in effecting a sudden shift from the "darker" to the "brighter" realm; in Ex. 13-10 the extremity of the flat side has been reached with the B and G minor triads; the interpolation of the A chord throws us back toward the sharp area.

FIGURE 13-2   Coloristic gamut of modal harmonies

(sharp/brighter)   (flat/darker)

E	A	D	G	C	F	B♭	(E♭)
			Em	Am	Dm	Gm	(Cm)

EXAMPLE 13-10

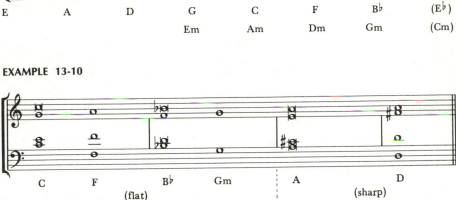

C   F   B♭   Gm   A   D
       (flat)   (sharp)

As may be surmised from the above discussion, the overall harmonic characteristics of this style are somewhat difficult to describe.[3] It is certainly not functional in the common-practice sense, although one will often find what amounts to a "IV-V-I" progression occurring at many cadence points. Alternations between relative major and minor "keys" (what LaRue terms *bifocal tonality*) are common. The overall tonal feeling is one of extreme restlessness, with only the cadences serving to stabilize the movement momentarily. The student should try to become familiar with as many examples from the literature as possible in order to gain some innate sense of the harmonic style before attempting to simulate it. The short response in Ex. 13-11 is included as a typical instance of a homorhythmic piece of this period. Note the contrary and parallel octaves in measures 9 and 16-17; the latter occurs after a cadence. Parallels between phrases, however, are not unusual since the offending intervals belong to different and unconnected elements.

ASSIGNMENT

Write a short composition in familiar style for four voices. Choose a section of text from the Gloria or Credo of the Ordinary (see appendix 2). You may use a condensed score on only two staves if you wish. Include well-defined

[3]For a further discussion of the harmonic aspects in this period see Andrew C. Haigh, "Modal Harmony in the Music of Palestrina," in *Essays on Music in Honor of Archibald Thompson Davidson, by His Associates* (Cambridge, MA: Department of Music, Harvard University, 1955), pp. 111–20.

cadences with typical suspension formulas at the end of each phrase. Bear in mind that these are usually followed by a rest before the next phrase resumes.

EXAMPLE 13-11

Marc Antonio Ingegneri: *Omnes amici mei* (Response)

Om- nes a- mi- ci me- i de- (de) re-

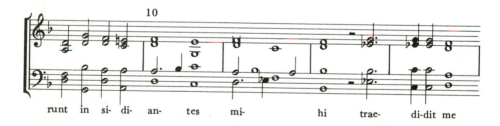

re- li li- que- runt me et prae- va- lu- e-

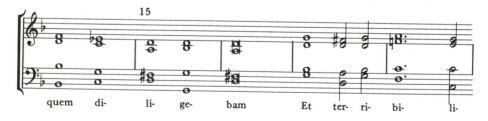

runt in si- di- an- tes mi- hi trae- di-dit me

quem di- li- ge- bam Et ter- ri- bi- li-

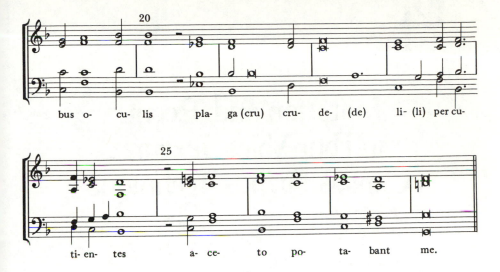

bus o- cu- lis pla- ga (cru) cru- de- (de) li- (li) per cu-

ti- en- tes a- ce- to po- ta- bant me.

14

Imitation and Reentry in Four-Voice Texture; Cantus Firmus Technique

In addition to discussing various imitative and reentry procedures typical of four-voice texture, a consideration of the second method of basing polyphonic pieces on preexistent material, that of *cantus firmus* technique, will be undertaken.

IMITATION AND REENTRY IN FOUR-VOICE TEXTURE

In general, those observations made in chapter 10 with respect to points of imitation and subsequent reentry in three-voice counterpoint, hold true for four-part writing as well. Fifth-relationships common to each particular mode continue as the basic organizing feature. While asymmetrical entrances in the initial point of imitation may still be observed, the even number of voices now available allows the possibility of two other frequent techniques, both of which involve a pairing of adjacent voice parts: two vs. two. In the first type of *paired imitation* the second voice enters relatively quickly at the usual fourth or fifth. The two initial parts then continue for some time in two-voice counterpoint, often cadencing immediately prior to the entrance of the remaining parts. The other voices then enter in exactly the same relationship as the first pair, completing the point of imitation. Ex. 14-1 illustrates this procedure with the respective pairs of voices brack-

EXAMPLE 14-1

Johannes Hahnel (Galliculus): Secunda Pars from *Evangelium in die Paschae*
(Motet from the Proper of his *Ostermesse*)

eted; note that the *tenor* drops out momentarily after measure 5 to prepare
the dovetailing cadence with a new theme at the end of the excerpt.[1]

A further instance is shown in Ex. 14-2. This passage reveals de
Monte at his most flamboyant; observe the use of only one minim distance
between paired voices.

This pairing technique may be noted also in four-voice canonic writing, producing a *double canon* (4 in 2) between the pairs of voices. Although
it will seem initially that all of the parts are involved with the imitation of
the *same* subject, eventually one of the pairs will break away and proceed
on its own course. Study the passage shown in Ex. 14-3 in this regard.

[1]For an additional example of this device see Ex. 17-1.

EXAMPLE 14-2

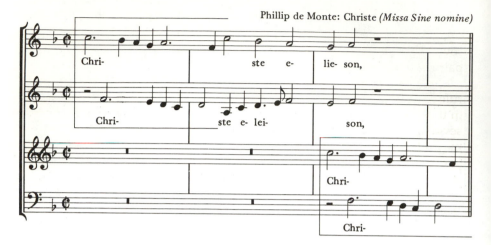

Phillip de Monte: Christe *(Missa Sine nomine)*

EXAMPLE 14-3

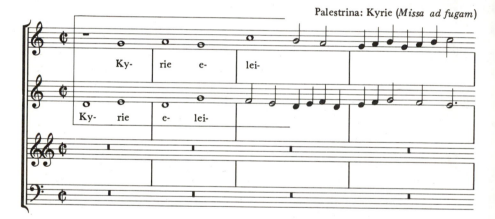

Palestrina: Kyrie *(Missa ad fugam)*

Another common device is the employment of what amounts to a *double-subject*. Here the initial two voices are not related thematically, but form a miniature segment of free counterpoint. The following double entry, reiterating the pitch classes of the original pair, will then occur after several measures, as shown in Ex. 14-4. In both of these techniques the pairing usually takes place between *cantus-altus* and *tenor-bassus*.

As discussed previously in chapter 10, subsequent reentries will, as a rule, continue to employ the same pitch classes of the fifth-relation found in the opening point of imitation. It is customary to rest a voice for at least several semibreves before bringing it back in with a reentry. Some latitude may be observed from a tonal and rhythmic standpoint in comparing the various reentries to the original subject, although the same text setting is usually preserved.

EXAMPLE 14-4

Palestrina: Kyrie (*Missa Lauda Sion*)

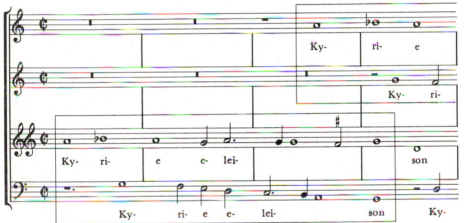

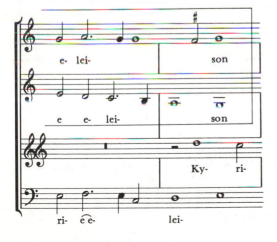

ASSIGNMENT

Write an opening point of imitation in four-voice texture using the text supplied below. You may wish to employ one of the paired procedures discussed above. Continue the counterpoint for at least six measures past the last entrance. Include a minimum of one reentry.

Ký-   ri-   e   e-   léi-   son
    (Lord   have mercy)

CANTUS FIRMUS TECHNIQUE

The technique of placing a chant melody in the *tenor* and composing successive counterpoints above it is one of the earliest procedures in the history of polyphony. In the medieval period the rhythmic structure of the *tenor* chant was determined by one of the so-called *rhythmic modes*. By the fifteenth century the melody was usually presented in long notes of equal value or *cantus planus* style. It might even appear in the *cantus* voice (*discant cantus firmus*), sometimes in a slightly embellished fashion.[2] In the sixteenth century the use of *cantus firmus* technique as the basis of Mass composition was in decline. Nevertheless, there are a sufficient number of works in this genre for us to devote our attention to the basic principles involved.

In a typical *cantus firmus* Mass of this period, each movement is based on a preexisting melody, either in whole or in part. The "tunes" employed as the *cantus* (or *soggetto*) can be either of sacred or secular origin. In addition to various examples of plainsong, Protestant chorales, secular melodies (sometimes derived from polyphonic compositions), and even abstract subjects may be found.[3] Two frequent examples may be cited; the folk song *L'Homme armé*[4] and the tones of the Guidonian hexachord.

The *cantus firmus* is normally located in the *tenor* voice (hence the term *tenor Mass*), although the discant style alluded to above is not uncommon. It is usually presented in longer note values than the accompanying counterpoint, frequently in breves or longs. The durations do not have to be of consistent length, although it is unusual to discover several short values

[2]Perhaps the definitive work on *cantus firmus* procedure in the fifteenth and early sixteenth centuries may be found in Edgar H. Sparks, *Cantus Firmus in Mass and Motet, 1420-1520* (Berkeley: University of California Press, 1963).

[3]Yet another source is the so-called *soggetto cavato*, in which the vowels of a phrase of text are extracted and transformed into a melodic line using syllables of the solmization system. For instance the *cantus firmus* employed in Josquin's *Missa Hercules Dux Ferrariae* is derived from the vowels of the title (Re Ut Re Ut Re Fa Mi Re). Also see Ex. 15-5.

[4]The opening phrase of this tune is given in Ex. 15-4.

within the context of the longer notes. Sometimes the *cantus* is repeated in a movement, with successively shorter values. As a consequence of the length of the *cantus* notes, it is often difficult, if not impossible, to identify the tune by simply listening to the work; this may account for the fact that composers were able to "hide" blatantly secular melodies within the polyphonic fabric of the Mass. Although the *soggetto* may open a movement, it usually makes its entry after the other voices have been established. If the *cantus* consists of fairly short phrases, rests will normally appear between the separate phrases. In most cases, the original text associated with the *cantus* tune is substituted with the words of the Mass.

By the Late Renaissance, the initial point of imitation opening a movement and the succeeding points of imitation are sometimes based on thematic elements of the *cantus*, resulting in a kind of *vorimitation* technique.[5] If this technique is employed, one must resort to the procedure of paraphrasing discussed in chapter 11. However, it is possible to find many instances where the counterpoint has little or no relation to the *soggetto*. A typical example of the former "paraphrase" approach is illustrated in Ex. 14-5. The *tenor* carries the five-note motive, which occurs in longs. Note the cadence just prior to its entrance.

EXAMPLE 14-5

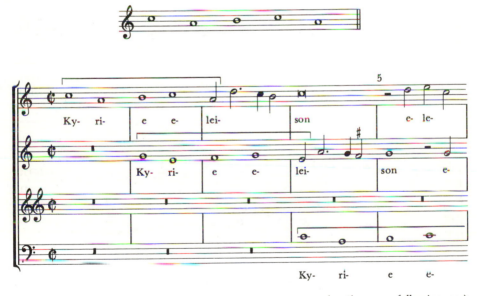

(continues on following pg.)

---

[5]An excellent example of this procedure may be found in Soderlund and Scott, *Examples of Gregorian Chant*, p. 220.

EXAMPLE 14-5   (*continued*)

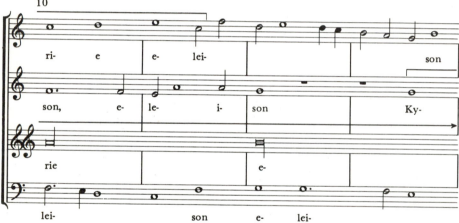

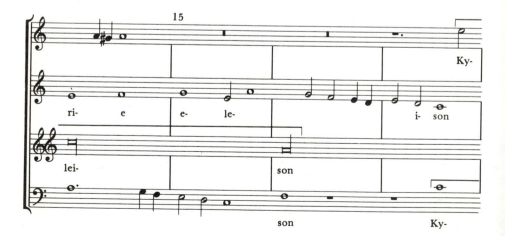

In Ex. 14-6 the *cantus* is the familiar hexachord mutated to G (*durum*). As it occurs at the opening of the piece in fairly short values, Palestrina proceeds to compose a counterpoint to it, thereby creating an example of double-subject imitation discussed previously.

EXAMPLE 14-6

Palestrina: Crucifixus (*Missa Ut Re Mi Fa Sol La*)

(continues on following pg.)

EXAMPLE 14-6 *(continued)*

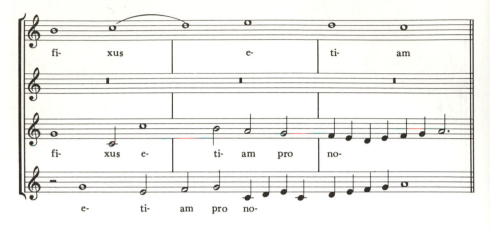

Two additional problems warrant our attention. One is the matter of chord choice as related to the harmonic rhythm. Obviously, the long notes of the *cantus* limit the number of possible consonant sonorities in the harmony. The problem lies in knowing how to vary the harmony sufficiently during each different *cantus* note duration. One must resort to chord connections involving common-tone relations, such as fifth- or third-relations, the "common tone" in each case being the *cantus* note. If the *soggetto* pitch is G, the harmonies could be G major, C major, or E minor. Root movement by second, therefore, becomes possible only between changes of the *cantus* pitches, or while the *cantus* is "resting" between phrases.

The other problem concerns the subsequent subject reentries following the opening point of imitation. As the *cantus* will doubtless be sounding throughout most of each phrase, the reentries must be counterpointed against its sustained tones. This often requires some degree of ingenuity. Refer back to Ex. 14-5 as regards both of these situations.

In composing a *cantus firmus* movement it is probably useful to make a preliminary sketch first. This should contain the *cantus*, laid out in consecutive phrases with appropriate rests in between, the initial point of imitation (perhaps based on the *cantus* in paraphrase style), points of imitation at the beginning of each new phrase, and any examples of reentries. Once this sketch has been completed, the missing voices may then be supplied. One such preliminary draft is given in Ex. 14-7. The *cantus* employed here consists of the first two phrases of the familiar Thanksgiving hymn, *We Gather Together*.

EXAMPLE 14-7

(continues on following pg.)

EXAMPLE 14-7   *(continued)*

(Cantus)

ASSIGNMENT

Choose a tune for use as a *cantus*. It may be any tonal melody that you wish, although those with basic stepwise motion generally work out better. It should consist of two short melodic phrases, not more than about eight notes per phrase. Although your tune need not be modal itself, consider the first and last tones of each phrase as regards an appropriate modal setting. Place it in the *tenor* voice and proceed to write a brief *cantus firmus* movement around it using the text below. Base your opening point of imitation on the *cantus* melody, employing paraphrase technique; the other point of imitation for the second phrase may be constructed on the second phrase of your tune although it need not be. Work in at least one reentry during each phrase, counterpointing it against the *cantus* voice. It will probably be helpful to make a sketch first, similar to the one in Ex. 14-7.

Sańc-   tus,   Sańc- tus, Sańc- tus, Dó- mi- nus Dé- us
  (Holy,   Holy,   Holy,   Lord   God

Sá-   ba- oth.
  of Hosts)

15

Examples
of Four-Voice
Compositions for Analysis

The eight compositions included in this chapter range in complexity from pieces that incorporate the abstruse canonic techniques found near the end of the fifteenth century (Ex. 15-6) to those which incorporate procedures of the Venetian school (Ex. 15-7) at the close of the century.

EXAMPLE 15-1:   Heinrich Isaac: *Innsbruck, ich muss dich lassen* (Lied - c.1515).

The first two examples in this chapter are secular pieces in the vernacular languages of German and French respectively. The melody of this basically homophonic setting was later used for several chorale texts, including Hesse's *O Welt ich muss dich lassen,* which was harmonized by Bach and Brahms. Composed about 1515, it is typical of the Flemish tradition carried on by such figures as Lassus. Examine the piece for doublings, spacing, and cadential formulas.[1]

---

[1]A linear analysis of the lied appears in Saul Novak, "Fusion of Design and Tonal Order in Mass and Motet: Josquin Desprez and Heinrich Isaac," *Music Forum,* 2 (1970), pp. 236–37.

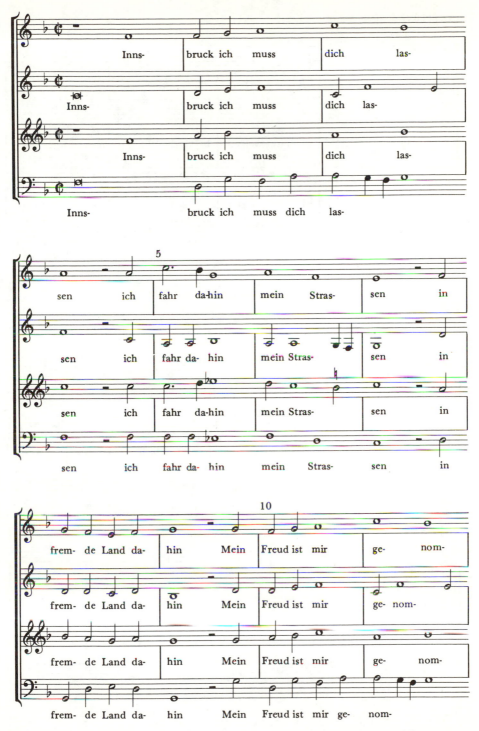

(continues on following pg.)

EXAMPLE 15-1   *(continued)*

Inns- bruck, ich muss dich las- sen, ich   fahr   da- hin mein Stras-sen,
(Innsbruck,   I   must you leave, I am going   on   my   way,

in   frem- de Land da- hin. Mein Freud ist   mir   ge- nom- men,
into   a foreign Land.   My   joy   is from me   taken,

die ich nit   weiss be- kom- men, wo ich im E- lend bin.
it   I know not how   to regain,   while I in misery am.)

EXAMPLE 15-2:   Lassus: *Bon jour mon coeur* (French chanson 1571).

This well-known secular composition is an excellent example of familiar style used in this period. Study the work with regard to those characteristics of this procedure discussed in chapter 13: spacing, inversion, doubling, and harmonic root movement. Observe the close relationship of the
text to the musical setting.[2]

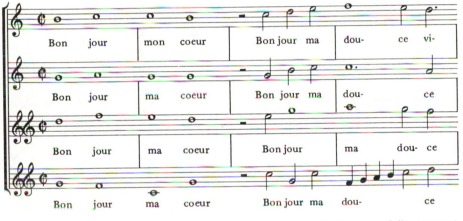

(continues on following pg.)

[2]An excellent analysis of this piece may be found in Robert Cogan and Pozzi Escot,
Sonic Design: The Nature of Sound and Music (Englewood Cliffs, NJ: Prentice-Hall, Inc., 1976),
pp. 130–41. The opening section of a keyboard transcription of Lassus' chanson by the English
composer Peter Philips is quoted in Archibald Davidson and Willi Apel, *Historical Anthology of
Music* Vol. I (Cambridge, MA: Harvard University Press, 1949), pp. 159–60.

EXAMPLE 15-2 *(continued)*

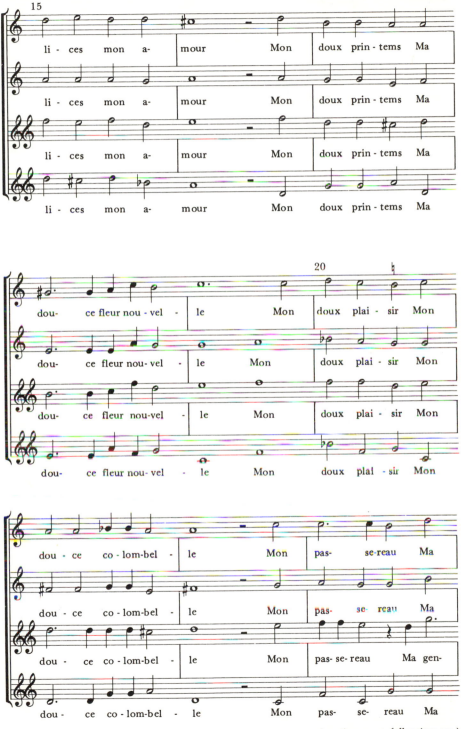

(continues on following pg.)

EXAMPLE 15-2 (*continued*)

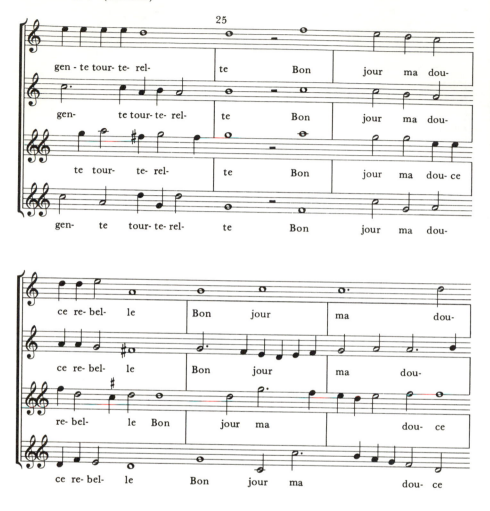

Bon   jour mon coeur. Bon jour ma dou- ce vie, Bon jour mon oeil,
(Good day my heart, good day my   sweet life, good day my eye,

Bon   jour ma che- re a- mi- e, He! bon jour ma tout- te bel- le, Ma mig- nar- di-se,
Good day my dear friend, Ah! good day my lovely one, my   sweet one,

Bon   jour mes de- li- es, mon a- mour, Mon doux prin- temps,
Good day my delight, my   love,   my sweet springtime,

Ma dou- ce fleur nou- vel- le, Mon doux plai- sir,
My   sweet flower   new,   my sweet pleasure,

Ma dou- ce co- lom- bel- le, Mon pas- re- reau, Ma gen- te tour- te- rel- le!
My sweet   dove,   my   lark,   my fair   turtledove!

Bon   jour ma dou- ce re- bel- le.
Good day my sweet   rebel.)

EXAMPLE 15-3: Palestrina: Excerpt from the Gloria of his *Missa brevis* (1570).

The condensed style of this "short mass" offers a model example of the quasi-homorhythmic writing often encountered in the long movements of the Ordinary, the Gloria and Credo. The Gloria is customarily divided into two large sections, the first beginning with *Et in terra pax* (the opening of the movement, *Gloria in excelsis Deo*, is intoned by the priest), the second with *Qui tollis . . .* [3] Only the first part is illustrated here. Observe the new thematic ideas and changes of texture that occur with each successive phrase of text.

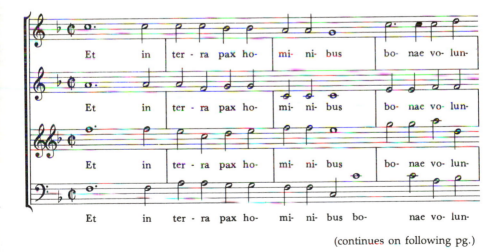

(continues on following pg.)

[3]Each of these two large sections might also be subdivided, in turn, into shorter musical movements.

EXAMPLE 15-3   *(continued)*

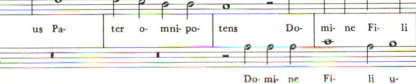

(continues on following pg.)

EXAMPLE 15-3 (*continued*)

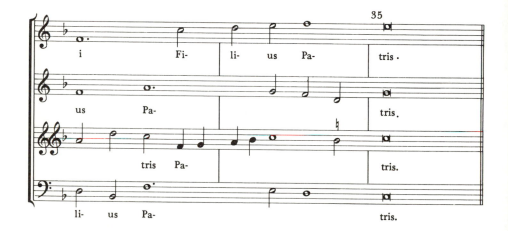

Et   in ter- ra pax ho- mi- ni- bus bo- nae vo- lun- ta- tis
(And on earth peace   to men   of good   will

Lau- da- mus te. Be- ne- di- ci- mus te. Ad- o- ra- mus te.
 We praise you.   We bless you.   We adore you.

Glo- ri- fi- ca- mus te. Gra- ti- as a- gi- mus ti- bi pro- pter mag- nam
 We glorify you.   Thanks   we give   to you for   great

glo- ri- am tu- am. Do- mi- ne De- us, Rex cae- le- stis,
 glory   your.   Lord   God, King of heaven,

De- us Pa- ter om- ni- po- tens, Do- mi- ne fi- li u- ni- ge- ni- te
 God the Father omnipotent,   Lord   Son the only begotten

Je- su Chri- ste, Do- mi- ne De- us, A- gnus De- i, Fi- li- us Pa- tris.
 Jesus Christ,   Lord   God, Lamb of God, Son of the Father.)

EXAMPLE 15-4: Palestrina: Opening section of the Benedictus from his *Missa L'Homme armé* (1570).

Three different instances of *cantus firmus* treatment are quoted in the following examples. As mentioned in the discussion of this technique, the folk song *L'Homme armé* became a model *cantus* in the *tenor* Masses of the fifteenth and sixteenth centuries, in which composers attempted to demonstrate their technical prowess. The opening phrase of the tune is quoted above the Benedictus; observe how Palestrina has rhythmicized the *cantus* in such a way as to preserve the basic ternary meter of the folk song. Although the first neighboring motive of the point of imitation does not relate to the *cantus*, the initial five tones of the *qui venit* do show their derivation. In addition to the subsequent reentries, note the curious static passage in measures 19-20, with the voice exchange in the inner parts.

(continues on following pg.)

EXAMPLE 15-4   *(continued)*

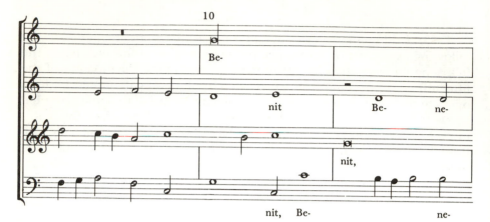

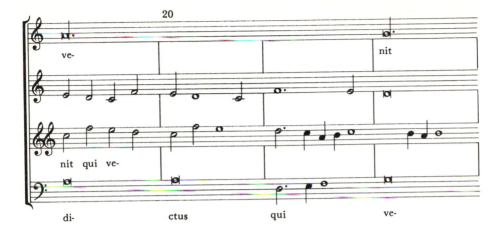

EXAMPLE 15-5: Josquin: Opening section of *Vive le Roy* (Uiue le Roi) for instruments (1503).

An instrumental work in four-voice texture, this fanfare-like movement demonstrates the unusual combination employing *cantus firmus* technique within the framework of a strict, three-voice asymmetrical canon. Only the opening section is quoted; the *cantus* is transposed a fifth higher in the next part and then reappears at the original pitch level. Study the harmonic aspects of this piece; why do you think there is such a preponderance of root movement by third? Given only the music and its title, can you ascertain the origin of the *cantus firmus*?

(continues on following pg.)

EXAMPLE 15-5   *(continued)*

EXAMPLE 15-6:   Christopher Tye: *In Nomine* (c.1550?).

Examples of *In nomine* instrumental pieces are very common among the English composers of the Late Renaissance. The term refers to the setting of the phrase *in nomine Domini* in the Benedictus of Taverner's Mass *Gloria tibi Trinitas,* which employs this section of the chant as a *cantus.* Here, the plainsong is set again in the upper voice in discant style. Although the opening subject is not related to the *cantus,* it is developed intensively during the course of the first section. Why do you think the triadic motive is particularly compatible here?

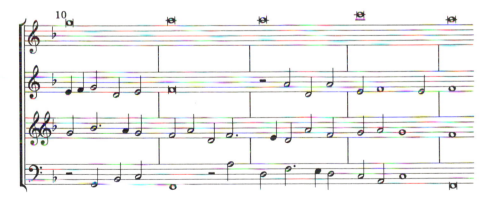

EXAMPLE 15-7:   Andrea Gabrieli: Kyrie from his *Missa brevis* (c. 1570?).

A highly compressed movement, this Kyrie is typical of the motivic style of the Venetian school. Note the canzona-like rhythm of the last section with its numerous reentries. Can you find any stylistic deviations from the contrapuntal principles presented thus far?

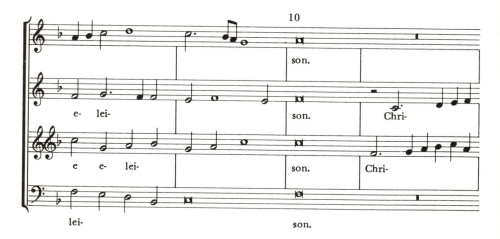

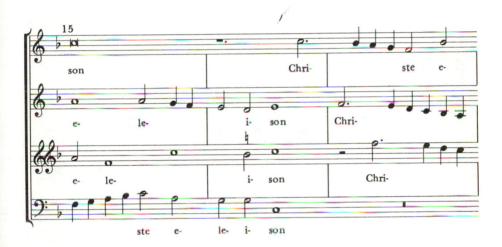

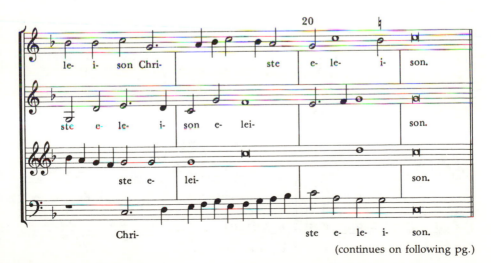

(continues on following pg.)

EXAMPLE 15-7   (*continued*)

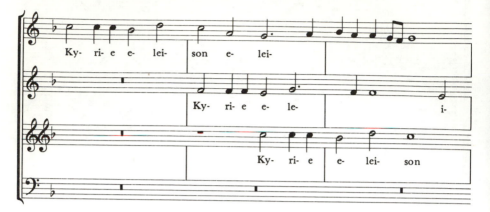

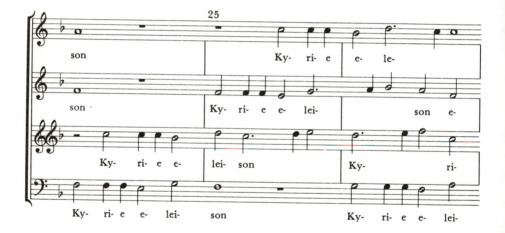

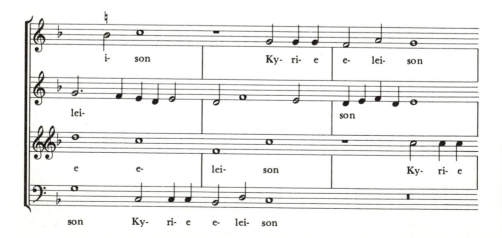

16

Aspects of Five- and Six-Voice Texture; Triple Meter

Examples of five- and even six-voice texture are quite common in the sacred polyphony of the Late Renaissance. The treatment of this number of voices will be discussed in this chapter. The use of triple meter as it pertains to the rhythmic structure of the music in this period will also be investigated.

BASIC FEATURES OF
FIVE- AND SIX-VOICE WRITING

Most of the following presentation will deal specifically with five voices. A concluding paragraph will consider the features characteristic of six-voice texture.

The "additional" voices are denoted numerically by *quintus* and *sextus*. They are usually either *tenor* or *cantus* parts. In strict five-voice writing, triads are invariably complete, although doubling procedures may vary widely. Excessive unison doubling is avoided in favor of octave doubling, producing the fullest possible sound. The doubling of raising *musica ficta* is still forbidden; this holds true for suspension dissonance as well. There is great latitude in the spatial arrangement of the parts; however, large gaps between consecutive upper voices are rare. Although parallel perfect intervals are still avoided, one may occasionally note the use of fifths by contrary motion in six-voice texture. The restrictions regarding the approach to octaves and even unisons are more relaxed than in writing for four voices. Study Ex. 16-1 in relation to the above observations.

EXAMPLE 16-1

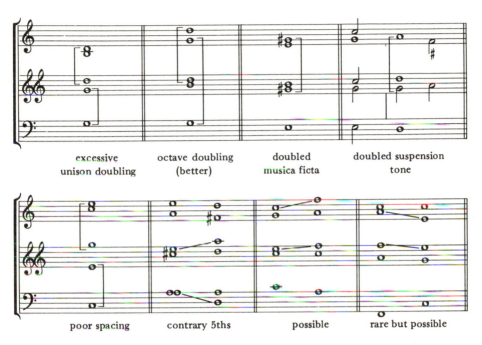

excessive unison doubling	octave doubling (better)	doubled musica ficta	doubled suspension tone

poor spacing	contrary 5ths	possible	rare but possible

The most frequent cadence is the 4-3 authentic formula, probably because the resulting fifth-relation involves the fewest voice-leading problems. Notice the doubling in Ex. 16-2A and B; the latter features a typical *cambiata* figure. The consonant fourth-device in Ex. 16-2C doubles the fourth, with the G in the second *tenor* acting as a kind of "consonant auxiliary." The root movement by fifth in the plagal cadence also presents a minimum of part-writing difficulties (Ex. 16-2D). However, the leading tone and Phrygian formulas are slightly more problematic, as no common tones exist. Notice the doubling and consequent voice-leading in Ex. 16-2E through G. The leaps in the latter two examples are necessary in order to avoid the doubling of the *musica ficta* in the final chord. Ex. 16-2H is not possible, because of the resulting parallel fifths.

Finally, one instance of a $^6_5$ has been included in Ex. 16-2I.

In a typical five- or six-voice movement, less than one-third of the music actually employs the maximum number of voices. The texture tends to be the most dense during the conclusion of the points of imitation and near the approaches to the cadences. Homorhythmic sections are also quite

EXAMPLE 16-2

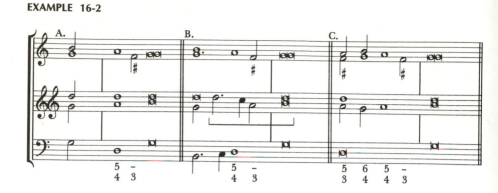

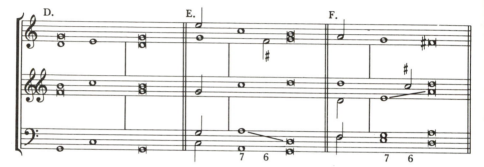

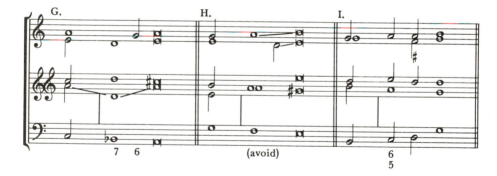

full. Within the interior of the phrases, however, the voices are in a continual state of textural flux, usually varying between three or four parts. Apparently, one of the main reasons composers favored a larger number of voices was the great degree of textural variety afforded them. Consult Ex. 18-2 in particular, regarding the preceding remarks. In points of imitation, the concept of fifth-relation still prevails. During the opening sections the temporal distances between entering voices is often asymmetrical, with the final part delaying its entry for some time. On the other hand, opening *stretto*-like imitations are not uncommon, in which the voices enter so rapidly that the thematic identity of the initial subject is frequently obscured. Contrast the rather leisurely exposition of voices in Morales' motet (five voices in eleven measures) illustrated in Ex. 16-3, with the rapid entry of parts in Palestrina's famous *Missa Papae Marcelli* (six voices in six measures) shown in Ex. 16-4.

EXAMPLE 16-3

Morales: *O Crux ave, spes unica* (motet)

(continues on following pg.)

EXAMPLE 16-3 (*continued*)

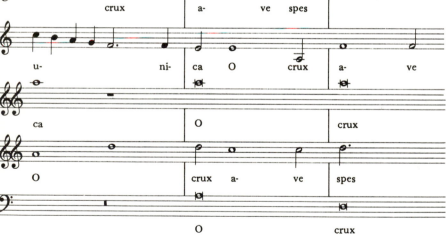

EXAMPLE 16-4

Palestrina: Kyrie (*Missa Papac Marcelli*)

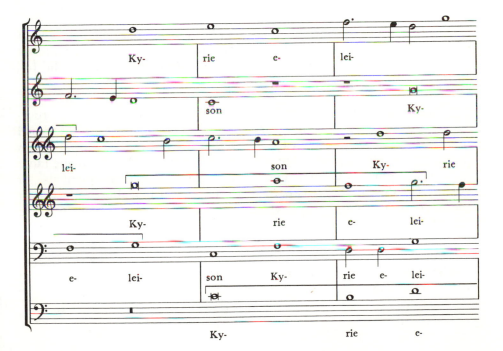

In five- or six-voice compositions it is not unusual to find a movement with as many as three parts beginning simultaneously at the opening, either in familiar style or treated in quasi-imitation with several free voices. Observe the beginning of Ex. 18-3D.

There are no strikingly different features in six-voice texture. Obviously, as each new voice is added, the problems of voice-leading and the resultant possibilities of parallels become more acute. Several instances of typical six-part cadences are shown in Ex. 16-5.

EXAMPLE 16-5

ASSIGNMENT

Write an opening point of imitation for five voices based on a text of your choice. Once all the parts have entered, continue the complete texture for at least four to six more measures to experience the "feel" of the full texture.

Because of the extensive use of interrupted and dovetailing procedures, interior cadences often cease to function as obvious points of formal and tonal punctuation, with the result that the music tends to take on a seamless quality. The working out (or "development") of thematic ideas within the phrases is often intense and complex, with frequent use of *stretto*. For this reason, it is particularly important that those subjects for points of imitation be chosen which lend themselves to multiple imitative situations, both tonally and temporally. In passages of this nature it may be best to "sketch out" first those voices reentering with the basic thematic idea of a phrase, and then to proceed to "fill in" the remaining contrapuntal texture. Study the following such sketch in Ex. 16-6, which consists of only the imitative reentries of the subject.

EXAMPLE 16-6

Analyze the thematic "development" in the closing section of the following *Credo,* which is based on a single descending minim motive (Ex. 16-7). Note the pitch classes used for reentry and the various temporal distances between imitations.

EXAMPLE 16-7

Palestrina: Credo (*Missa Papae Marcelli*)

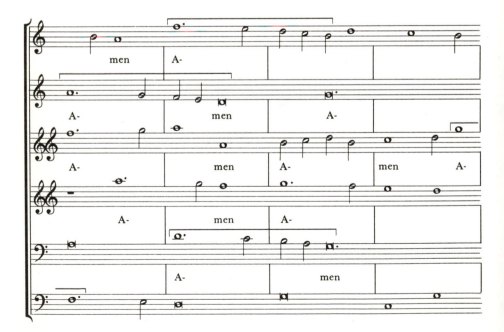

ASSIGNMENT

Using the theme in Ex. 16-8 (or one of your own choice), write about ten measures of an interior phrase in five voices. Strive for a maximum number of reentries, but try to limit your initial pitch classes to a single fifth-relation (C and G or C and F in the example below). Incorporate as many different tonal relations and temporal distances between the voices as you can. It is not necessary to retain all five voices continually; in fact, each reentry should be preceded by a rest.

EXAMPLE 16-8

in glo- ri- a (De- us Pa- tris)

TRIPLE METER

So far, the only metric scheme considered in this text has been that of *alla breve* ¢ (2/1, or considering the minim as the "beat," 4/2). Triple meter occurs less commonly than imperfect time in the sacred polyphony of the sixteenth century. Individual movements composed entirely in triple meter will be considered first. They may be grouped roughly into two basic categories: (1) those with a "slow tempo," in which the beat remains the minim (∂ = approximately 96 M.M.), and (2) those in which a longer note value receives the beat or "fast tempo."

In slow tempo there are also two possibilities, depending upon how the breve is divided and subdivided in the time and prolation system of the period. In *alla breve* the division of the breve is by two (*Tempus imperfectum*) and the division of the semibreve is also by two (*Prolatio imperfecta*):

In slow triple meter the "beat" is still the minim, but other divisions of the breve are now employed:

Tempus perfectum (X3)
Prolatio imperfecta (X2)

Tempus imperfectum (X2)
Prolatio perfecta (X3)

In the first case, the meter signature is written Φ. Thus, the meter may be thought of as 3/1, or a grouping of 2 + 2 + 2 minims. The only difference between this meter and *alla breve* is the addition of two "extra" beats per measure. The rhythmic placement of consonance and dissonance is not affected, so that the prevailing rules of strong and weak occurrence continue in effect. Suspensions may now appear on beat 5, minim passing tones on beat 6, etc. Examine the short excerpt in Ex. 16-9, noting the handling of dissonance.

In the second case, the meter signature is written as $\bigcirc$ $\frac{3}{2}$, thus partitioning the breve into two "measures" of 3/2 each or 3 + 3. The minim still remains the unit of beat. However, strong beat dissonances, such as the suspension or $\frac{6}{5}$, may now occur on any beat; before cadences they generally fall on the second minim. Study the brief illustration in Ex. 16-10.

Slow tempo triple meters can usually be recognized quickly by the presence of black-note values. It should be noted in passing that both of the above situations are somewhat rare in this period.

EXAMPLE 16-9

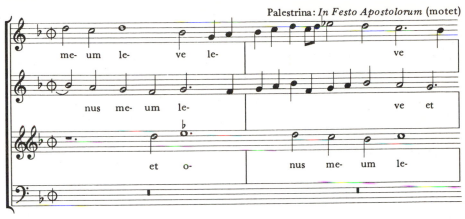

EXAMPLE 16-10

In "fast tempo" meters the prevailing beat is now the semibreve, producing a perfect division of the breve (|o| = o o o). The note values, in terms of the handling of consonance and dissonance, have been doubled in duration in that the semibreves are now equivalent to what were previously minims, minims to semiminims, etc. The commonly encountered texture is that of familiar style, with the result that there is very little use of nonharmonic tones. Typical examples may be found in settings of the Hosanna and in polychoral compositions. However, composers may sometimes resort to purely polyphonic procedures in this meter. Suspensions (in semibreves) usually occur on the second beat; there is no occurrence of semibreve passing or neighboring tones; these must now be minims. The use of *hemiola* (three breves spread over two measures) may be seen, particularly before cadences.[1] The homorhythmic excerpt in Ex. 16-11 is taken from the opening of a polychoral work.

EXAMPLE 16-11

Palestrina: *Veni Sancte Spiritus* (motet)

[1]See Michael B. Collins, "The Performance of Sesquialtera and Hemiola in the 16th Century," *Journal of the American Musicological Society*, 17 (1964), pp. 5-28.

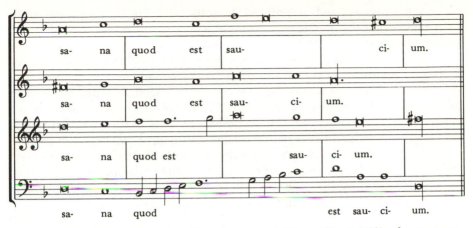

In the Hosanna passage from a canonic Mass (Ex. 16-12), the texture features imitation that results in a double canon between *cantus-altus* and *tenor-bassus*. Analyze the nonharmonic functions of the minims, observing the *hemiola* near the end.

EXAMPLE 16-12

Palestrina: Hosanna (*Missa ad fugam*)

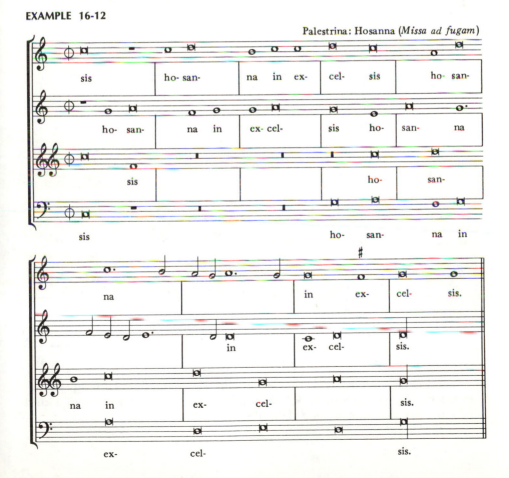

The prevalent use of long, white-note durations may lead one to the conclusion that this music progresses at a very slow pace. In actuality, the semibreve is roughly equivalent to the minim of *alla breve* and may even be taken at a faster rate. The effect is sometimes almost "scherzo-like" in nature and justifies the use of the term "fast tempo."

Another situation involves the change of meter from duple to triple *during* the course of a single movement. This technique sometimes occurs near the end of some motets of the period. In cases of this nature it is generally acknowledged that a *proportional* relationship exists between the meters, in that the minim does *not* remain constant. The proportions are usually 3:1 or 3:2. In Ex. 16-13, the semibreve in the triple meter is now three times faster than before. The proportional relations are shown at the top of the example, with their equivalents in modern notation.

EXAMPLE 16-13

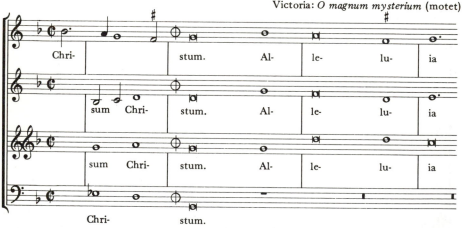

Ex. 16-14 illustrates a 3:2 relationship. Note that meter change occurs in the middle of a measure. Both examples would seem to represent a kind of Renaissance "metric modulation"!

EXAMPLE 16-14

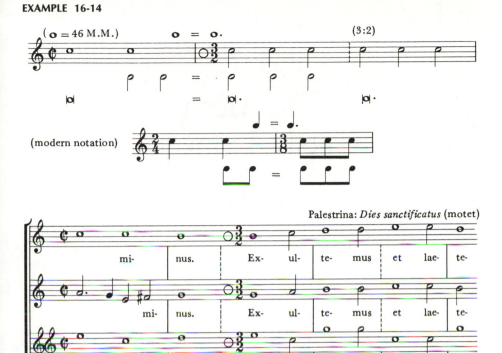

Palestrina: *Dies sanctificatus* (motet)

Any practical writing assignments using triple meter will be post-poned until after the discussion of polychoral techniques in chapter 19.

17

The Motet;
Parody Technique

This chapter will present the structural aspects of the motet of the sixteenth century and the process of parody technique, the last remaining procedure in which Mass movements are based on preexistent material.

THE MOTET

The motet (*motetus*) represents one of the most common genre of sacred composition in the Late Renaissance. Although any short sacred or scriptural writing could serve as a suitable text, most of the literary sources for the motet are found in the Proper of the Mass, which changed from Sunday to Sunday according to the liturgical year. In contrast to the Ordinary, which remained constant, the Proper presented a vast repertory of possible texts. Indeed the challenge of setting new texts may have appealed to certain composers, who found the Ordinary too confining.

It is outside the scope of this text to go into the long history of the derivation of the term motet, and the subsequent evolution of this type of composition.[1] Suffice to say that it was the important developments in the motet during the fifteenth century that laid the foundations of "through-

---

[1] A brief history of this genre may be found under "Motet" in Willi Apel, *Harvard Dictionary of Music*, 2nd ed. (Cambridge, MA: Harvard University Press, 1969), pp. 541-45.

imitative" style so typical of the Late Renaissance. A cursory review of motet structure is in order, although in principle the form is essentially identical to that of *sectional through-composition* discussed earlier in chapter 6. The text is divided into short phrases, each of which is assigned its own distinguishing thematic material. Points of imitation customarily introduce each phrase, although contrasting homorhythmic sections may be found. After the usual "development" through reentries, the phrases conclude with some type of cadential punctuation. This process is repeated until the last phrase is finished. Although certain similarities of thematic construction between sections may be occasionally observed, examples of the return of actual thematic material from earlier phrases are rare.[2] A notable exception is the so-called "responsory" motet (aBcB). An interesting though unusual instance of thematic return can be found in Palestrina's great motet *Alleluia tulerunt*, quoted in Ex. 18-2. Here the opening *Alleluia* section is briefly "recapitulated" between the phrases of text and is finally expanded at its conclusion, giving the work a kind of "rondo" effect.

Motets were often divided into two large separated sections, denoted as *prima pars* and *secunda pars* (or first and second parts). It is not uncommon to find a concluding section written in triple meter using familiar style. Although most motets are original compositions, some use of paraphrase procedure involving chant melodies may be observed. Two complete motets are shown in chapter 18.

PARODY TECHNIQUE

The basing of movements of the Ordinary of the Mass on a preexistent polyphonic composition, resulting in a so-called *parody Mass* (or *missa parodia*), is extremely common in the Late Renaissance.[3] Indeed, about half of Palestrina's hundred-odd Masses employ this process. The previous work may be either sacred or secular in nature; usually motets or chansons are used. The composer might "borrow" either one of his own earlier pieces or that of another composer, as nothing approximating copyright laws existed. In fact a lesser composer might have felt flattered to have one of his pieces deemed worthy enough for a renowned master to base one of his Masses upon it.

---

[2]In this regard see Oliver Strunk, "Some Motet Types of the 16th Century," *Papers read at the American Musicological Society 1939* (1944), p. 155.

[3]Two excellent surveys of this procedure may be found in Lewis Lockwood, "On 'Parody' as Term and Concept in 16th-Century Music," *Aspects of Medieval and Renaissance Music*, ed. by Jan LaRue (New York: W. W. Norton and Company, Inc., 1966), pp. 560–75, and Quentin W. Quereau, "Aspects of Palestrina's Parody Procedure," *Journal of Musicology*, 1 (1982), pp. 198–216. Also, see John Ward, "Parody Technique in 16th-Century Instrumental Music" in *The Commonwealth of Music in Honor of Curt Sachs*, ed. by Gustave Reese and Rose Brandel (New York: The Free Press, 1965), pp. 208–28.

The actual technique of parody is quite varied.[4] In some cases, whole sections are lifted intact with only the text changed. In other instances, the basic thematic material is all that is employed. Sometimes the major cadential points and overall tonal schemes are retained, while in other cases a complete structural and tonal reworking is made.

There do seem to be some prevailing tendencies with respect to how the various sections or separate phrases of the original composition are distributed throughout the Mass. Each major division of the Mass (Kyrie, Gloria, etc.) begins with a reworking of the *initial* section of the preexisting piece. Each successive subdivision of the movements then parodies the consecutive phrases of the original work. If we number the sections of a hypothetical motet I, II, III, etc., then the opening Kyrie will be based on I, the Christe on II, and the last Kyrie on III. If the motet is in two parts, the opening of the *secunda pars* will often occur at major structural divisions of the Gloria or Credo.

Although it is in only four-voice texture, Palestrina's Christmas motet *Dies sanctificatus* will serve as a model.[5] Its initial two sections are quoted in Example 17-1. The opening point of imitation presents a classic instance of paired imitation. The text of the first phrase is divided into two short subphrases, with each assigned its own thematic idea. Note that subsequent reentries feature only the second idea (see measures 14-16). After a cadence on G in measure 17 (the mode is Mixolydian), the second phrase *renite gentes* begins in the *bassus*, with subsequent imitations in the *altus* and *tenor*.

EXAMPLE 17-1

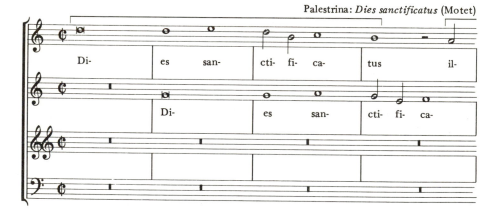

Palestrina: *Dies sanctificatus* (Motet)

---

[4]Several interesting analyses based on an original system may be found in Quentin W. Quereau, "Sixteenth-Century Parody: An Approach to Analysis," *Journal of the American Musicological Society*, 31/3 (1978), pp. 407–41.

[5]This motet and the subsequent mass based upon it are also discussed in Jeppesen, *Counterpoint*, pp. 241–61 and Soderlund, *Direct Approach*, pp. 126–7.

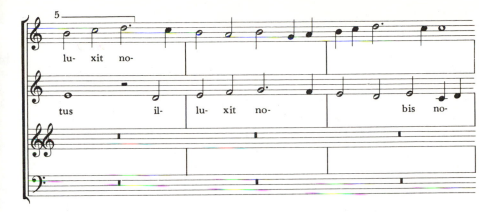

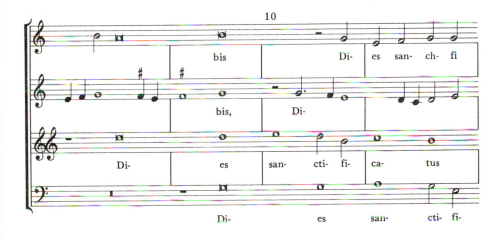

(continues on following pg.)

EXAMPLE 17-1   (*continued*)

Two excerpts from his parody Mass based on this motet follow in Ex.
17-2 and 17-3. In the Kyrie, exact quotations from the motet are enclosed in
brackets. In general, the *illuxit nobis* theme with its ascending tetrachord
has been developed further through additional reentries (see measures
13-15), although measure 7 of the motet has been omitted altogether. The
initial entries of the *tenor* and *bassus* are shifted forward by one semibreve,
an excellent example of cadence overlap. Note the reworking of the final
cadence.

The Agnus Dei II is based on the *renite gentes* motet theme (section II, beginning in measure 18). The texture has been expanded to five voices, with the added *altus* forming a canon at the fourth with the *tenor*. By slightly modifying the theme tonally and rhythmically, Palestrina is now able to effect a *stretto* imitation between the *cantus* and *altus* I. This pairing appears in the later entries of the *tenor* and *bassus*. The movement represents a complete reworking of the motet material with little but the original theme retained.

EXAMPLE 17-2

Palestrina: Kyrie (*Missa Dies sanctificatus*)

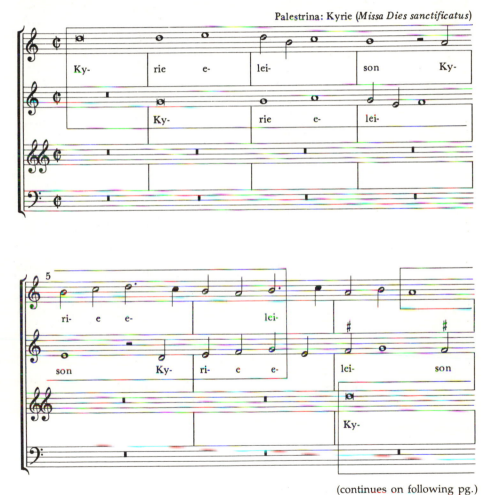

(continues on following pg.)

EXAMPLE 17-2   *(continued)*

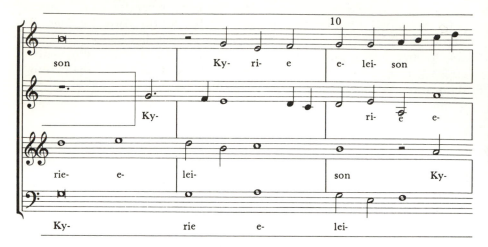

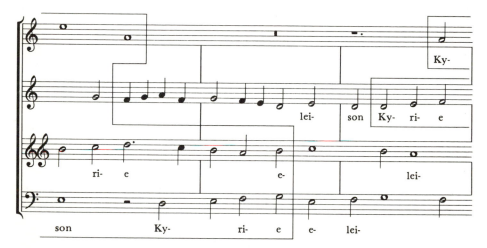

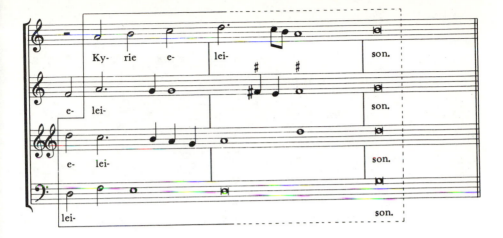

EXAMPLE 17-3

Palestrina: Agnus Dei II (*Missa Dies sanctificatus*)

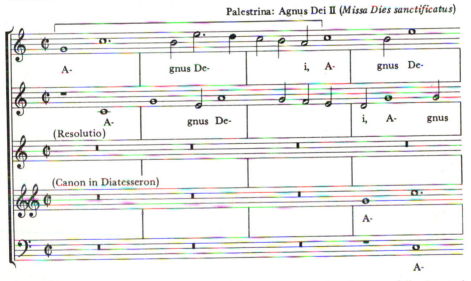

(continues on following pg.)

EXAMPLE 17-3   *(continued)*

Two additional instances of parody technique appear in Ex. 18-3 and 4 of the following chapter.

ASSIGNMENT

Using the first section of the Victoria motet quoted in Ex. 17-4, write a five-voice Kyrie employing parody technique. As in the case of the previous Palestrina motet, the text has been divided and each subphrase given a distinctive motive (*Iste sanctus, pro loge Dei sui*). The *tenor* and *bassus* entries omit the rest between the two ideas. Note the varied reentries on *pro loge* in measures 11-12, using diminished values and a tonal adjustment. The mode is transposed Mixolydian with a final cadence on C.

In your parody realization you may wish to retain the composer's original point of imitation, although a fifth entry must now be appended. The *tenor* reentry in measure 9 could serve this purpose well. Extend the length of the excerpt beyond its original duration; for subsequent reentries you may wish to "develop" the *pro loge* theme. It is possible to retain much of Victoria's cadence. Use only the *Kyrie eleison* text and write for two *tenor* voices.

EXAMPLE 17-4

Victoria: *Iste sanctus* (motet)

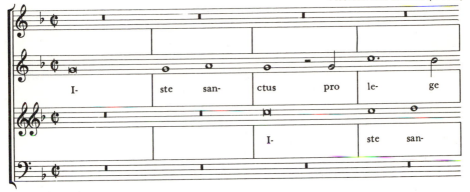

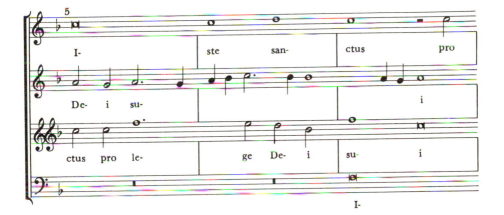

(continues on following pg.)

EXAMPLE 17-4   (*continued*)

18

Examples
of Five- and Six-Voice
Compositions for Analysis

In addition to the first two motets illustrated in this chapter, there are several excerpts of Mass movements employing parody technique, which are shown with their original sources. The last example incorporates six-voice texture.

EXAMPLE 18-1: William Byrd: *Terra tremuit* (motet 1607).

Although the text of this brief work is taken from the Easter Mass, Byrd does not paraphrase the chant melody itself; see Ex. 1-3 for a reproduction of the original plainsong. The musical settings of its three sections are closely allied to the words. The remarkable word painting in the opening phrase gives way to the rich chordal texture of the middle part. The final *Alleluia*, with its intense imitative procedures, is typical of many of the composer's sacred works.

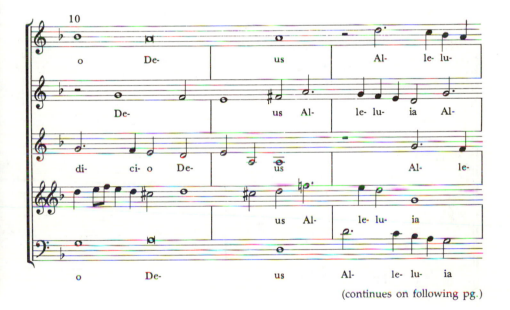

(continues on following pg.)

EXAMPLE 18-1   *(continued)*

Ter- ra   tre- mu- it, et qui- e- vit.
(The earth trembled, and was still.

dum re- sur- ge- ret in ju- di- ci- o De- us. Al- le- lu- ia.
when   arose   in judgement God.)

EXAMPLE 18-2:   Palestrina: *Alleluia tulerunt* (motet 1569).

This magnificent piece is yet another example using the Proper of the Easter Mass. In this case, the text is taken from John's account of the Resurrection (20:13,15). The composer has added an *Alleluia* and treated its polyphonic setting in a cyclic fashion, thereby giving the motet a kind of "rondo-like" structure. Compare the opening and closing sections based on the *Alleluia* material, as well as the brief interludes between the phrases. In particular, observe the manner in which each different phrase is handled, with respect to texture. Do you see any similarities between the thematic material of the various phrases?

(continues on following pg.)

ci- to mi-

hi

di- ci- to

di- ci- to mi-

hi

um di- ci- to mi-

hi di- ci- to mi-

um

di- ci- to mi-

di- ci- to mi-

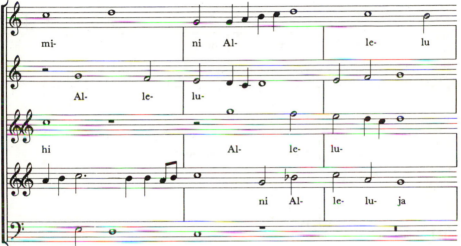

mi-

ni Al-

le- lu

Al- le- lu-

hi

Al- le- lu-

ni Al- le- lu- ja

hi

ja

et e- go e- um

ja Al- le- lu- ja

et

ja

et e- go e-

Al-

le- lu- ja

et e- go

Al- le- lu- ja

EXAMPLE 18-2   *(continued)*

(Al- le- lu- ja) Tu-   ler-   unt Do- mi- num me- um,   et   ne- scio u- bi
               (They have taken   Lord   my,   and I know not where

po- su- e- runt e- um. Si tu su- stu- li- sti e- um, di- ci- to mi- hi,
    they laid Him.   If you have taken away Him,   tell   me,

et   e- go tol- lam.   (Al- le- lu- ja).
and   I   will take Him.)

EXAMPLE 18-3: Palestrina: Opening section of his motet *Memor esto* (1572); Corresponding sections found in the Kyrie, Gloria, Sanctus, and Agnus Dei of his *Missa Memor esto* (1599).

The opening sixteen measures of the motet (Ex. 18-3A) represent the initial point of imitation using the first phrase of text. Analyze this section carefully, noting the two thematic ideas associated with *Memor esto* and *verbi tui servo tuo*. Then trace how this material has been parodied in the beginnings of four movements of the Mass (Ex. 18-3B through E).

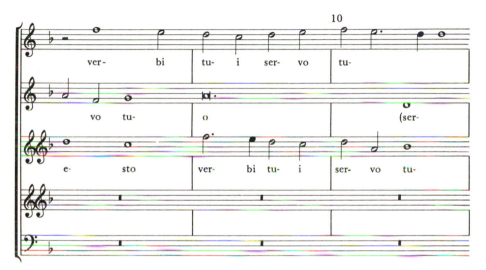

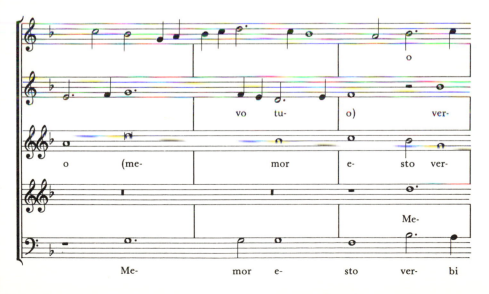

EXAMPLE 18-3 (*continued*)

Me-mor   e-sto   ver-bi   tu-i   ser- vo   tu- o.
(Remember   Word   your   servant   to your)

15

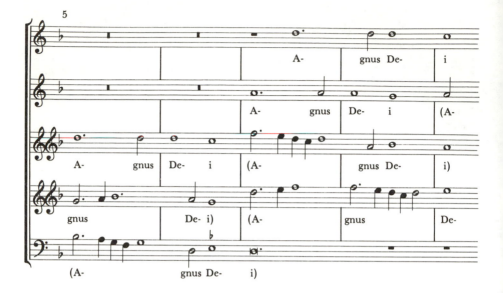

EXAMPLE 18-4: Palestrina: Opening sections from *Pars I* and *II* of his motet *O magnum mysterium* (1569); corresponding sections in the Kyrie and Agnus Dei II from *Missa O magnum mysterium* (1582).

This Christmas text was a favorite of composers of the late sixteenth century. The well-known motet of Victoria is one of many examples.[1] Palestrina's six-voice motet is in two "parts"; only the opening measures of each are quoted (Ex. 18-4 A and B). The initial sections of the Kyrie and Agnus Dei II in the parody Mass are modeled after these two parts, respectively (Ex. 18-4C and D). Here the parody technique is more involved than that found in the *Memor esto* movements. Do a careful analysis of those elements which are retained and modified in the Mass, and note the inclusion of any new material.

[1]Victoria's motet and the *Kyrie* to his Mass are quoted in Gordon Hardy and Arnold Fish, *Music Literature: A Workbook for Analysis*, Vol. II (Polyphony) (New York: Dodd, Mead & Company, 1967), pp. 220–26. In addition to the Palestrina excerpts illustrated here, four other settings by sixteenth-century composers are cited in William Brandt, et al, *The Comprehensive Study of Music: Anthology of Music From Plainchant through Gabrieli*, Vol. I (New York: Harper & Row, Pub., 1980): Willaert (pp. 178–84), Victoria (pp. 222–24), Byrd (pp. 225–30), and G. Gabrieli (pp. 236–42). The chant for this Christmas responsory may be found on page 15 of that anthology.

A. (Motet)

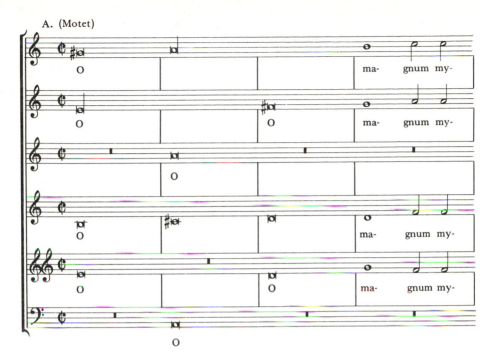

(continues on following pg.)

EXAMPLE 18-4   (*continued*)

O ma- gnum my- ste- ri- um et ad- mi- ra-bi- le sa- cra- men- tum.
(O great   mystery   and admirable   sacrament.)

(continues on following pg.)

EXAMPLE 18-4   (*continued*)

B. (Motet) Secunda Pars

(Secunda Pars)
Quem vi- di- stis, pa- sto- res? di- ci- te.
(What did you see, shepherds? Tell us.)

(continues on following pg.)

C. (Mass) Kyrie

(continues on following pg.)

EXAMPLE 18-4   *(continued)*

D. (Mass) Agnus Dei II

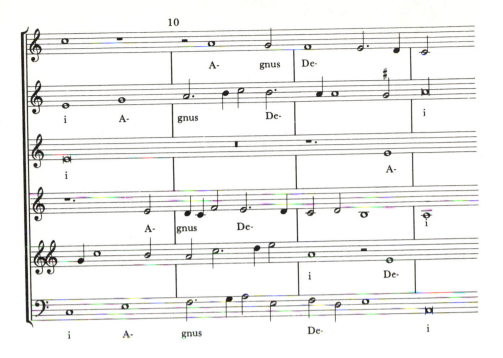

19

Eight-Voice Texture; Polychoral Style

In those choral textures featuring an even number of voices, composers frequently divided the parts into two equal forces that were played against each other. In some of his four-voice works, Josquin, for instance, employed pairs of voices answering in a quasi-antiphonal manner. In the opening Kyrie of his *Missa ad fugam* (see Ex. 14-3), Palestrina divided his double canon (4 in 2) between *cantus-altus* and *tenor-bassus*. De la Rue's *Missa Ave sanctissima Maria* begins in a similar fashion, except that here the texture is for six voices, dividing the triple canon between pairs of three parts each (6 in 3).[1]

By about the middle of the sixteenth century, the Venetians were experimenting with the use of two separate choirs (called *coro spezzato* or broken-choir style). Some historians have speculated that this may have resulted from the presence of two choir lofts in St. Mark's cathedral in Venice. Willaert, Andrea Gabrieli, and later his nephew Giovanni Gabrieli were the main figures in cultivating this technique. The usual number of parts was eight (4 + 4) or twelve (4 + 4 + 4) voices, although even larger forces were sometimes used. This method of textural distribution was quickly adopted by other composers of the period. It is interesting to note

[1]This work is quoted in Charles Burkhart, *Anthology for Musical Analysis*, 2nd ed. (New York: Holt, Rinehart & Winston, 1972), pp. 23–6.

that this procedure may well represent the first conscious exploitation of spatial (or stereophonic) effect in the history of music.[2]

Although the ways of using this technique are quite varied, the usual procedure consists of beginning the work with the separate choirs answering each other in alternation or antiphonal style. A typical opening is illustrated in Ex. 19-1.

EXAMPLE 19-1

Palestrina: *Veni Sancte Spiritus* (Motet - opening)

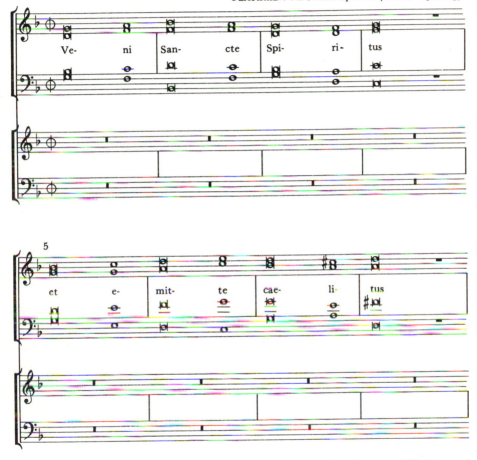

(continues on following pg.)

[2]Very little literature exists in English on the historical evolution and compositional characteristics of the polychoral style of the Late Renaissance.

EXAMPLE 19-1 (*continued*)

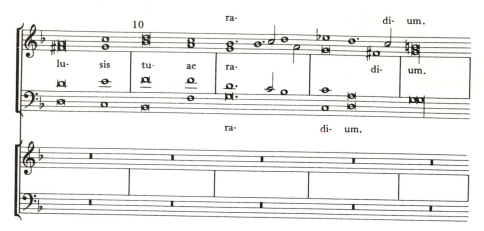

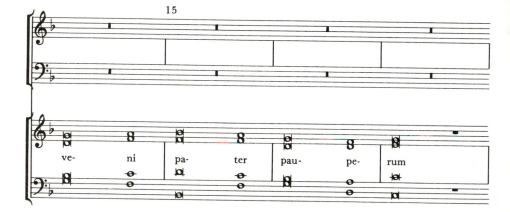

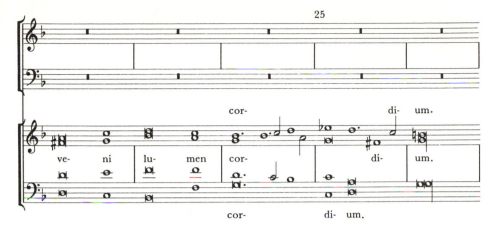

As the piece continues, some overlapping between the forces, particularly at cadence points, will be seen until, near the end, both choirs eventually join together, thus giving the impression of an overall tightening or *stretto*. In this regard consult Ex. 19-2.

EXAMPLE 19-2

Palestrina: *Veni Sancte Spiritus* (Motet - conclusion)

(continues on following pg.)

EXAMPLE 19-2   *(continued)*

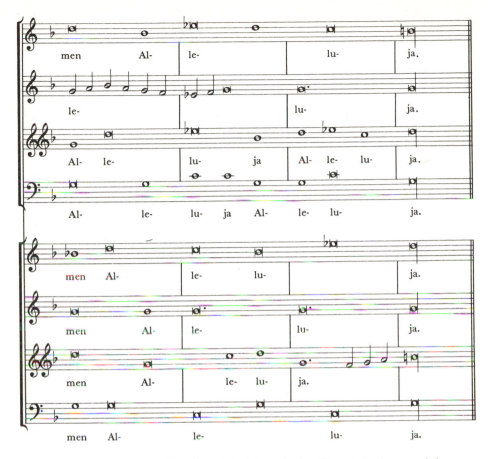

Palestrina's motet *Veni Sancte Spiritus,* in familiar style, is a model case in point.[3] The text is based on a hymn by Innocent III; it consists of five stanzas of six lines, each in strict poetic meter. In the first four strophes Choir I presents the opening half of each stanza, followed immediately by Choir II with the second half, but in an identical musical setting (refer to Ex. 19-1). Beginning with the fifth stanza, there is a shortening of phrases for the individual choirs, with some overlapping at cadences. Finally, all the forces join in the last few lines, concluding with a short "coda" based on *Alleluia Amen* (see Ex. 19-2 above). The structural chart in Fig. 19-1 outlines the basic features of this work, denoting stanzas, phrase lengths, and cadences. Observe how Palestrina extends the final part of every third line by one measure to avoid the periodic repetition of four-measure phrasing.

[3]This motet is included in Gustave Soderlund, *Examples of Gregorian Chant and Works by Orlandus Lassus, Giovanni Pierluigi Palestrina, and Marc Antonio Ingegneri,* 3rd ed. (New York: Appleton, Century, Crofts Inc., 1946), pp. 36–43, but was omitted by Samuel Scott in his subsequent revision of this anthology.

FIGURE 19-1 Structural Diagram of Palestrina's *Veni Sancte Spiritus*

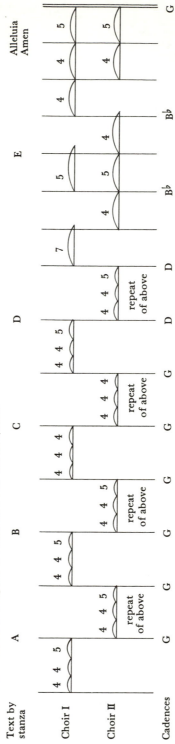

A few general observations dealing with the handling of eight-voice texture follow. Here the basic problem in voice-leading is the avoidance of parallel perfect intervals, which continue to be forbidden. Composers employ three different devices to circumvent their occurrence. These are illustrated in Ex. 19-3: (1) contrary octaves or fifths, particularly common between the pair of *bassus* parts, which often simply interchange pitch classes by contrary motion, (2) voice-crossing, usually in the inner voices (see *altus* II and *tenor* II), and (3) the use of rests between chord changes (see *cantus* II and *tenor* I).

EXAMPLE 19-3

The doubling of raising accidentals is still avoided, although it may occasionally be noted between overlappings, or at final cadences, involving a raised third of the chord. The doubling of the suspension and resolution in 4-3 cadences is also forbidden. Cadential formulas are restricted to the authentic (4-3 suspensions) and plagal cadences, as both employ root movement by fifth-relation. Harmonic progression consists mostly of fifth-relations with some movement by thirds, as these allow the retention of common tones in the voice-leading. Root motion by second is particularly problematic, as no common tones exist. The resultant harmonic rhythm is usually slow in terms of the notation. Indeed, in eight voice texture it would appear that each chord change represents a new crisis in terms of the part-writing.

In familiar style, the sonorities are normally in root position, with the pair of *bassus* parts exchanging notes through contrary motion at chord changes. The chordal integrity of each individual choir is usually preserved and complete triads are used whenever possible, with normal spacing of the chordal members. Often, one choir may be written in basically close structure, while the other is in open structure. Excessive doublings at the unison between choirs are avoided; the sound is usually kept as full as possible. In this regard it is interesting to quote Zarlino: "Because the choirs are located at some distance from one another, the composer must see to it that each choir has music that is consonant, that is without dissonance among its parts, and that each has a self-sufficient four-part harmony."[4] Consult Ex. 19-4.

EXAMPLE 19-4

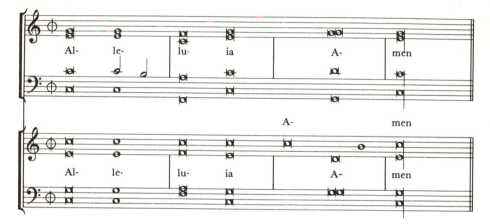

ASSIGNMENTS

Write the following cadences in an eight-voice double choir format. You may use a condensed score (two staves) for each choir.

1. Authentic cadence (with 4-3 suspension) in the Dorian mode
2. Plagal cadence in the Mixolydian mode (no suspension)
3. Just for fun, a Phrygian cadence in root position (What are the problems?)

Afterwards, write a short passage in familiar style of about four measures, illustrating some of the various techniques for avoiding parallel perfect intervals.

After carefully studying the excerpts of eight-voice writing in chapter 20, write a brief polychoral piece in eight parts using a condensed score. The meter should be 3/1, the fast triple meter discussed in chapter 16. The text may be Latin or English, as you desire; a hymn text will often work very well. It is usually better if the text is in a strict poetic meter so that the lines or stanzas are of equal length. An iambic meter (short-long) will work

[4]Gioseffo Zarlino, *Le Istitutioni harmoniche,* Part 3 (1558), trans. by Guy A. Marco and Claude V. Palisca (New York: W. W. Norton & Company, Inc., 1976), p. 243.

best in the triple rhythm. Begin the first unaccented syllable with a dotted breve in all parts at the opening. Structure the piece according to the model diagram in Fig. 19-1, although your work will be considerably shorter in duration. Begin with the typical antiphonal answering between separate choirs, gradually incorporate some cadential overlap, and eventually conclude with at least six to eight measures of eight-voice texture. Keep all nonharmonic activity to a minimum, as is customary in familiar style, with only occasional minim passing and neighboring tones and the usual 4-3 suspension at cadences.

20

Examples of Eight-Voice Compositions for Analysis

The examples cited in this chapter represent three varying ways of treating eight-voice texture.

EXAMPLE 20-1: Victoria: Agnus Dei from *Missa Simile est regnum caelorum* (1576).

The concluding movement of this interesting Mass is cast in the form of a strict canon between the two four-voice choirs (8 in 4). The continual antiphonal imitation and cadential overlap show the influence of polychoral technique. Only the last seven bars show consistent eight-voice writing. Note the major cadential points in terms of the mode. The little *tenor* "tailpiece" is curious.

EXAMPLE 20-2: Palestrina: Closing section from the motet *O Admirabile commercium* (date unknown).

The final section of this work for double choir is an excellent example of polychoral writing in triple meter. The prevailing style is homorhythmic. Again, note the typical dovetailing of cadential points. Analyze this piece from the following standpoints: (1) the root movement between chords in the eight-voice texture, (2) the use of nonharmonic tones in a fast triple meter, and (3) any instances of rests or contrary perfect intervals as means of avoiding parallels. Interestingly enough, there are three examples of parallels which Palestrina seems to have overlooked. Can you locate them?

EXAMPLE 20-2 *(continued)*

Lar- gi- tus est no- bis su- am de- i- ta- tem.
(He bestowed   on us   His   divinity.)

EXAMPLE 20-3:   Morley: Illustration of eight-voice writing from his *A Plain and Easy Introduction to Practical Music* (1597).

What compositional device is employed in this ingenious example? Does the composer manage to avoid all instances of parallel perfect intervals?

21

Additional harmonic Devices in the Late Sixteenth Century

Up to this point, the musical traits discussed have been typical of the sacred vocal writing of the Late Renaissance. However, near the close of the sixteenth century, a number of harmonic idioms appear which require examination. While most of these tend to occur in secular compositions, composers on occasion utilized them in their sacred works. They are most frequently encountered in the Italian madrigal, the English school, and in those works associated with the Venetian composers. One may note the occurrence of rather exotic *musica ficta* in many of the examples. A more thorough presentation of this tendency will be reserved for chapter 22.

Other Cadence Formulas

Several additional devices may be appended to the traditional cadence formulas. In Ex. 21-1A note the use of the semiminim escape note in conjunction with a consonant fourth, as well as the final passing seventh in the *tenor*. These traits were found with particular frequency in the music of the English school. Note the curious consonant fourth in Ex. 21-1B, creating a dissonance with the *altus*. It becomes increasingly common in the music of Venetian and Italian madrigalists.

EXAMPLE 21-1

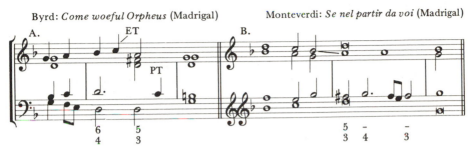

Byrd: *Come woeful Orpheus* (Madrigal)   Monteverdi: *Se nel partir da voi* (Madrigal)

Augmented Triad

Although seldom encountered in sacred works, the augmented triad, always in $_3^6$, may be observed in some secular pieces. Its most typical use is at cadential points in conjunction with a consonant fourth, employing an E♭ in place of the diatonic E♮ (Ex. 21-2A). In the second illustration it occurs as the result of the interaction of the D♯ and G♮ (Ex. 21-2B). As the excerpts show, this sonority is often employed as a "color chord" to highlight a text dealing with cruelty, pain, or death. Ex. 21-2C is very curious, with its clash between the E and F; observe the "escaped" upper G.

EXAMPLE 21-2

Gibbons: *The Silver Swan* (Madrigal)   Gesualdo: *Tu m'uccidi, O Crudele* (Madrigal)

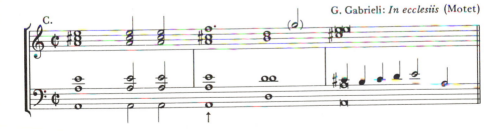

G. Gabrieli: *In ecclesiis* (Motet)

Augmented Sixth;
Diminished Sevenths

The chord of the augmented sixth finds its origin in this period. It can occur as the result of a suspension (Ex. 21-3A), a neighboring tone (Ex. 21-3B), or even a chromatic passing tone (Ex. 21-3C). Note the enharmonic spelling and use of the diminished third in the Gesualdo excerpts (Ex. 21-3C and D). Ex. 21-3E illustrates a diminished seventh chord, originating as a suspension with a change of bass. Both sonorities are extremely rare.

EXAMPLE 21-3

Cross Relations

Cross relations sometimes appear between the final cadence chord of an interior phrase and the opening of the next section. The major triad of the cadence will be followed by the same chord with a change of mode (or minor third); consult Ex. 21-4A. Cross relations may also occur in close proximity within the phrase as the result of the voice-leading of the parts involved. In Ex. 21-4B the respective B♮ and B♭ are both auxilaries. The cross relation in Ex. 21-4C is even more striking. Of special interest are those instances where the cross relation takes place simultaneously in the same sonority! Although this is typically identified with the English school, one occasionally encounters it in other styles.[1] In almost all cases the logic of the voice-leading prevails; a neighboring tone is usually involved (see Ex. 21-4D through F). It should be pointed out that the majority of cross-relations involve the chromatic alteration of either the 3rd or 7th scale degree of the mode.[2]

EXAMPLE 21-4

[1]For a discussion of this device as exemplified in the works of Byrd see Edmund Fellowes, *The English Madrigal Composers* (London: Oxford University Press, 1921), pp. 171–73.

[2]One is reminded of a similar tendency in American blues.

Pedal Point

Although more common in early organ works, the device of a pedal point is sometimes noted in certain secular vocal works as well (Ex. 21-5). Here the term implies the existence of unexplained dissonance in the upper voices above the pedal.

EXAMPLE 21-5

Gesualdo: *Io pur respiro* (Madrigal)

ASSIGNMENT

Carefully analyze the two following excerpts from Thomas Weelkes' madrigal *Oh Care, Thou Wilt Despatch Me*,[3] and note the frequent use of the consonant-fourth device occurring in various guises, as well as other harmonic points of interest. These passages are quoted in Ex. 21-6 and 21-7.

[3]This entire madrigal is quoted in Palisca, *Norton Anthology* Vol. I, pp. 269–72.

EXAMPLE 21-6

Thomas Weelkes: *Oh Care Thou wilt despatch Me* (Madrigal)

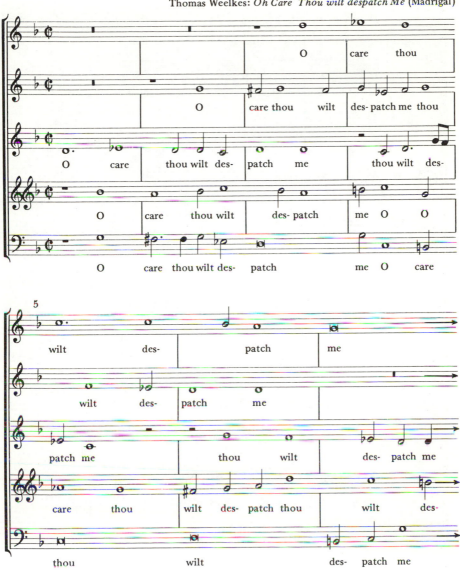

EXAMPLE 21-7

22

Extended Musica Ficta and Chromaticism

The latter half of the sixteenth century witnessed the emergence of two factors that would eventually contribute to the undermining of the modal system. The advent of functional tonality, with its correlated hierarchy of ordered modulatory relations finally culminating in the major and minor modes, begins to appear first in a germinal sense in the dance music of the Late Renaissance. It features a heavy reliance upon strongly periodic meter and phrasing with regularly recurring cadential punctuation, set in a fairly homophonic texture. On the other hand, its almost diametrically opposite trend, the use of extended *musica ficta* and chromatic voice-leading, was also explored by composers of the period.[1] This latter style gradually begins to appear in a variety of media and forms, eventually reaching its most extravagant expressions in madrigals and certain keyboard pieces near the end of the century. Although it made but slow inroads in the more conservative sacred style, this mannerism is nevertheless an important enough trend to include in our study, as it never really abandoned the basic contrapuntal idiom. As the topics of an extended system of accidentalism and linear chromaticism often go hand in hand, we will discuss only the former, at present.

The use of *musica ficta* has, to this point, been limited to a well-defined

---

[1]For a more elaborate presentation of these two opposing trends see Edward Lowinsky, *Tonality and Atonality in Sixteenth-Century Music* (Berkeley: University of California Press, 1961).

number of specific deployments (in this regard, review the opening of chapter 8). The employment of accidentals for the purpose of "coloristic" harmonic purposes was what first began to interest certain composers of this period. By extending the range of possible *musica ficta*, the basic chordal vocabulary was enlarged. Such notes as D♯, A♯, and E♯, and on the flat side A♭ and D♭, were incorporated in the existing repertory of sonorities, thus expanding the theoretical circle of perfect fifths:

(D♭ A♭) E♭ B♭ F C G D A E B F♯ C♯ G♯ (D♯ A♯ E♯)

Consonant triads such as B, F♯, C♯ A♭, and D♭ major, along with G♯, D♯, F, and B♭ minor, were now possible, as well as other augmented and diminished triads in the usual first inversion.[2] The sudden shifting from one end of the fifth-spectrum to the other by various third-relations or linear chromaticism produced violent harmonic contrasts not available heretofore. For instance, the B major and C♯ minor sonorities in the Lassus passage (Ex. 22-1A) create a striking relation to the diatonic opening; note the appropriate text setting (*Chromatico*).[3] The same two chords are reworked in the beginning of Gesualdo's madrigal (Ex. 22-1B), resulting in a Wagner-like progression by third-relations. The additional *musica ficta* also allow the further exploration of different and distinctive cadence formulas. Observe in Ex. 22-1C how the expected movement of the 7-6 suspension over F♯ does not resolve to an E triad but instead to an A $^6_4$, with the final cadence punctuation on a C♯ major triad! Macque's organ fantasy (Ex. 22-1D) does not incorporate any extended accidentals, but the frequent use of *musica ficta* for coloristic purposes creates novel and startling harmonic progressions, another byproduct of this technique.

EXAMPLE 22-1

Lassus: *Prophetiae Sibyllarum*

A.   (Car-   mi- na   Chro-   ma-   ti-   co)

---

[2]Lowinsky has speculated that these harmonic resources may have been present in the performance of certain pieces of a more diatonic nature, but that the exotic *musica ficta* was "hidden," rather than appearing in the actual notation. See his *Secret Chromatic Art in the Netherlands Motet* (New York: Columbia University Press, 1946).

[3]A linear analysis of this complete piece may be found in William Mitchell, "The Prologue to Orlando de Lasso's *Prophetiae Sibyllarum*," *The Music Forum*, 2 (1970), pp. 264–73.

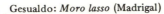

Gesualdo: *Moro lasso* (Madrigal)

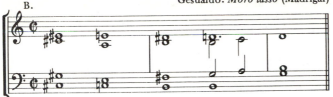

Gesualdo: *Resta di darmi noia* (Madrigal)

G. Macque: *Consonanze stravaganti* (for organ)

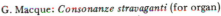

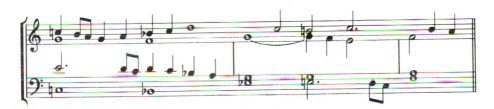

The results of chromatic voice-leading also served to enrich the harmonic palette of the composers in this period. The Lisztian third-relations in the Gabrieli passage (Ex. 22-2) are emphasized through the bold and stark textural treatment.

EXAMPLE 22-2

G. Gabrieli: *In ecclesiis* (Motet)

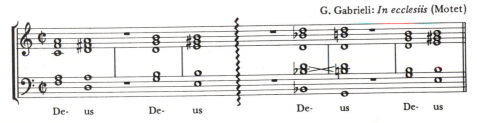

Linear chromaticism may appear in many guises in the hierarchy of a composition; as an isolated surface event, as an integral part of a thematic subject, or as the underlying constructive force in an entire movement. The choice of whether to employ a sharp or flat in the chromatic line is not arbitrary but dependent upon the intended harmonic background. Thus, a composer will use D-D♯-E when he wishes a B major chord, or D-E♭-E♮ when he employs a C minor triad. Similar situations are illustrated in Ex. 22-3. As these excerpts demonstrate, there is no abiding rule for using sharps in an ascending line or flats for a descending line.

EXAMPLE 22-3

Although the basic concept of fifth-relation is still in effect in points of imitation, two additional features of chromatic subjects may be noted. In order to create a more stable sense of tonality, many of the themes are framed by a movement from "tonic to dominant" or the reverse. The use of tonal answers involving these two tones is not infrequent; in regard to these points consult Ex. 22-4.

EXAMPLE 22-4

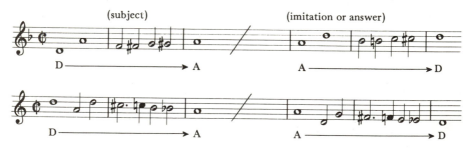

If the opening subject is chromatic in nature, one will often encounter a bona fide "countersubject" which is completely *diatonic*, thereby balancing the more ambiguous tonal sense of the first theme. The resulting harmonic intervals usually feature sequences of thirds and sixths, or their reverse. This accompanying counterpoint will frequently reappear with subsequent entries of the subject, usually in double counterpoint at the octave. For examples of this procedure consult Ex. 22-6 and 22-10. The number of theoretical harmonic situations arising from chromatic voice-leading is enormous. In actual practice the prevailing resultant progressions are somewhat more restricted. A few of the typical idioms encountered are cited below, pertaining to both falling and rising chromatic motion. It will be noted in most cases that the altered chromatic note usually falls on a weak beat (2 or 4).

In instances of descending chromatic motion Ex. 22-5A shows, perhaps, the most commonly encountered situation; here the flatted tones produce a series of falling stepwise first-inversion triads which change mode on the weak beat. Note the possibility of a 7-6 suspension in Ex. 22-5B. The next two illustrations feature root movement by third, with the second example again employing a suspension (Ex. 22-5C and D). Ex. 22-5E shows an instance of double chromatic inflection.

EXAMPLE 22-5

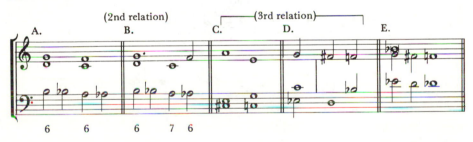

The opening measures of Monteverdi's *Crucifixus* (Ex. 22-6) are based on a subject spanning a tetrachord by descending chromatic motion. This device later became a well-known cliché, used in the baroque period to picture grief or pain. Indeed, Bach returned to this same idiom in his setting of the Crucifixus from his B minor Mass. Note the diatonic "countersubject" on the words *sub Pontio Pilato*. The scoring for men's voices alone gives an appropriately dark quality to the piece.

In rising chromatic motion the occurrence of fifth-relations is very frequent, where the mode of a minor triad is raised successively (Ex. 22-7A). Two instances of third-relation appear in Ex. 22-7B and C. Again the possibility of double inflection can be exploited (Ex. 22-7D and E).

EXAMPLE 22-6

Monteverdi: *Crucifixus*

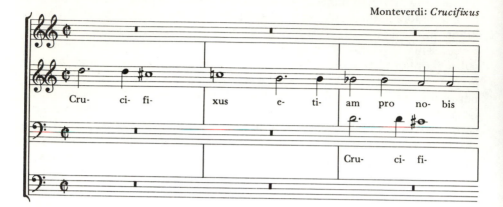

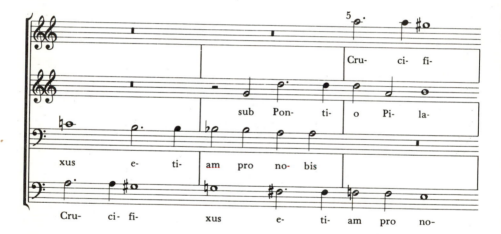

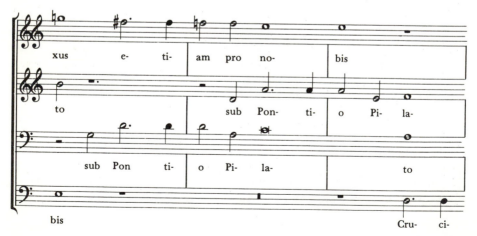

EXAMPLE 22-7

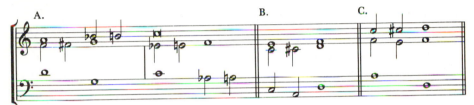

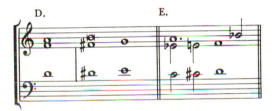

Ex. 22-8 cites the beginning of de Rore's *Calami sonum ferentes*, the setting of a Latin ode. The subject is almost completely chromatic in ascending motion; note the entrance on the tone B, ordinarily avoided as an initial note. Although this piece was written comparatively early in the century, it achieved widespread fame and apparently exerted an influence on later composers. Like the Monteverdi piece, it is scored for men's voices alone, in this case four basses![4]

Sweelinck's *Fantasy 1*, (probably written between 1590-1600) is based on a single descending chromatic tetrachord which is treated in extensive imitation, *stretto*, augmentation, and diminution. The chart in Fig. 22-1 dia-

[4]For an analysis of a chromatic work from this period see Kenneth Schmidt, "Harmonic Progressions in the Music of Gesualdo: An Analysis of *O Vos Omnes*," *In Theory Only*, 1/3 (1975), pp. 6–16.

EXAMPLE 22-8

de Rore: *Calami sonum ferentes* (Ode)

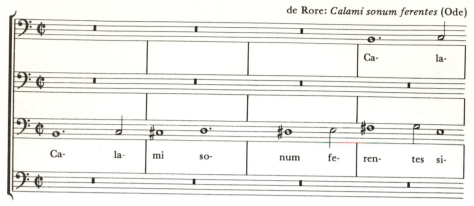

FIGURE 22-1 Structural Analysis of Sweelinck: *Fantasy I*   cadences

Section I (meas. 1–70)	Entries of Sub. ♩ on D, A with two counter-subjects (1 and 2) in triple cpt (Ex. 22-9A) (meas. 1–42)	Sub. ♩ entries on E (with 1) (meas. 43–55)	Stretto of Sub. ♩ on D and A (Ex. 22-9B) (meas. 55–70) D
Section II (meas. 71–118)	Entries of Sub. ♩ on A, D with 3, (Ex. 22-9C) followed by diatonic stretto and development of 3 (Ex. 22-9D) (meas. 71–94)	Point of imitation of 4 on D, A (Ex. 22-9E) followed by combination of Sub. o with 4 (Ex. 22-9F) (meas. 94–118) A	
Section III (meas. 119–149)	Entries of Sub. o on D, A with 5 in imitation with itself (Ex. 22-9G) followed by diatonic stretto of 5 (Ex. 22-9H) (meas. 119–139)	Short closing section based on quasi-stretto of Sub. o (A, D) (meas. 140–149) A	
Section IV (meas. 149–171)	Entries of Sub. ♩ at various pitch levels with 6 (Ex. 22-9I) (meas. 149–157)	Additional re-entries of Sub. ♩ at various pitch levels (meas. 158–171) A	
Section V (meas. 171–197)	Stretto of Sub. ♩ on A, D, G (Ex. 22-9J) (meas 171–183)	Closing section over pedals A and D with Sub. ♪ (Ex. 22-9K) (meas. 184–197) D	

grams the basic structure of the composition, noting the pitch classes at which imitation or reentry occurs, as well as its major divisions and cadential points. References are made in the figure to the musical excerpts in Ex. 22-9, in which the various counter-subjects Sweelinck employs against his original subject are bracketed and numbered. In extended works of this type it is interesting to note that composers balanced extensive chromatic sections with passages of a completely diatonic nature (for instance, see Ex. 22-9D, E, and H). The excerpts of Ex. 22-9 represent a virtual lexicon of the varied approaches to treating a descending chromatic subject.[5]

[5]The complete composition may be found in *Jan Pieters Sweelinck, Opera Omnia* Vol. I, ed. by Gustav Leonhardt (Amsterdam: Nirota Koedijk, 1968), pp. 1–6, as well as other practical editions.

EXAMPLE 22-9

(continues on following pg.)

EXAMPLE 22-9 *(continued)*

ASSIGNMENT

Write a short imitative monothematic piece for organ of from twenty to thirty measures in duration, based on a fully or partially chromatic subject. It should be scored for only three voices. Use two staves, and keep the upper two parts fairly close together to facilitate performance. A model opening point of imitation is given in Ex. 22-10. Incorporate several reentries of the subject, usually on the initial fifth-relation pitch classes. There should be at least one internal cadential punctuation. Try to work in an example of *stretto* near the end of the piece. Several such instances are shown in Ex. 22-11.

This chapter on chromatic style concludes our survey of contrapuntal practice in the Late Renaissance. As possible further areas of research one might investigate the literature of polyphonic chansons and their eventual incorporation in the instrumental canzonas near the end of the century, as well as other instrumental sources, such as the *ricercar*, fantasy, variation, and the English *in nomine* settings.

EXAMPLE 22-10

EXAMPLE 22-11

Appendix 1

Species Counterpoint

In 1725 Johann Fux published his epoch-making *Gradus ad Parnassum*, a counterpoint manual that quickly became the primary influence in polyphonic training for generations of composers to follow, including most of the major figures of the Classical period.[1] Although his knowledge of the music appeared, in light of later research, somewhat limited, he based his text on the style of the sixteenth century, and Palestrina in particular. His pedagogical approach was eminently logical; beginning with two-part writing, he had the student compose a counterpointing voice both above and below a given *cantus firmus* melody of semibreves. Fux's *cantus firmi* were original, and while predominantly stepwise in nature, they did not resemble the more usual chant tunes with their frequent repetitions of notes, that were actually employed by composers in the Renaissance.[2] The counterpointing voice was rigidly controlled with respect to its rhythmic and harmonic relation to the *cantus*, resulting in five distinct categories or *species*:

1. First Species: o against o
2. Second Species: 2 ♩ against o
3. Third Species: 4 ♩ against o
4. Fourth Species: syncopated ♩ against o
5. Fifth Species: "free" rhythmic values against o

[1] For bibliographical information and translations see the annotated bibliography.

[2] For instance, see the examples of *cantus firmi* used by Zarlino in Part Three of his *Le Institutione harmoniche*.

The student then proceeded to write free counterpoint in both voices, and followed that with exercises employing imitation and double counterpoint. This same species technique was then subsequently applied to three- and four-voice texture.

The species method is a valuable discipline in the study of counterpoint, in that it allows for a systematic approach to creating a melodic line, and the treatment of consonance and dissonance. It was these very qualities that led later theorists to seize upon the species technique as a logical tool in presenting general contrapuntal principles, as opposed to a more stylistic approach to the polyphony of the Late Renaissance. In particular, the species' close affiliation with layer analysis, in which compositions are reduced to a two-voice substructure of voice-leading, appealed to Schenker and his disciples. In addition to Schenker's own *Kontrapunkt* (vol. II of *Neue musikalische Theorien und Phantasien* 1906-35),[3] there are more recent texts in this same vein such as the Salzer-Schachter *Counterpoint in Composition* (1969) and Westergaard's *An Introduction to Tonal Theory* (1975). The use of species counterpoint in this manner, however, did not necessarily correspond to sixteenth century stylistic practice.

Indeed, there may be several drawbacks to the employment of a strict species approach in the simulation of the music of this period. Idiomatic devices, such as *portamento, cambiata*, accented passing tones, etc., are somewhat difficult to present within the context of third (quarter-note) species alone, and must wait until fifth species (or better still, entirely free two-voice counterpoint) is introduced. The rhythmic vitality (or microrhythm) of the Renaissance melody with its reliance upon the text is often neglected. The time needed for the systematic presentation of the species material may preclude the study of fuller, more common textures (for instance, five-voice polyphony) of the period, as well as certain compositional procedures, such as paraphrase or parody technique. The most successful text which orients the species approach to the practice of Palestrina and his contemporaries is Jeppesen's *Counterpoint* (1939); see the annotated bibliography at the end of this manual.

The examples of the various species below are taken from two sources, the Mozart-Attwood studies and theoretical treatises of the late sixteenth and early seventeenth centuries. The second section of the notebook Thomas Attwood compiled while studying composition with Mozart is devoted to a study of counterpoint in strict species approach.[4] In some instances Mozart merely provides excerpts from *Gradus* with minor changes (Fux's original counterpoint is given with notes in parentheses). All use the same Dorian *cantus* which was original by Fux.

It is not surprising that many of the counterpoint treatises of the Late

---

[3]This work is currently being translated by John Rothgeb and Jurgen Thym.

[4]The Mozart-Attwood studies are included as Serie X:30 in the *Neue Ausgabe Sämtlicher Werke* (Basel: Bärenreiter Kassel, 1982).

Renaissance employ a *cantus firmus* (or *discant*) approach, since this technique was quite prevalent in many of the Masses of the fifteenth century. What is interesting is that some of them (particularly those of Diruta, Banchieri, and Berardi) anticipate Fux's pedagogical method by including examples that closely resemble the order of species set down in *Gradus*. Almost all of them begin with a kind of first species note-against-note style (called *contrapunto semplice* or *punctum contra punctus*). The *cantus* melodies are either freely composed by the authors or perhaps taken from preexistent chants, although the sources are rarely quoted. Some of the treatises omit the intervening "species" and move directly to free style or fifth species (*contrapunto diminuto*). Any quasi-species approach is rarely maintained beyond two voices.

The restrictions in each species are briefly summarized; chapter numbers refer to detailed information given earlier in this manual. Some comments pertaining to the examples have been included.

I. First Species (1:1)

Only consonant intervals are allowed. See the section dealing with consonance in chapter 3.

Mozart's quotation of Fux's example, shown in Ex. 1, contains one minor alteration near the cadence. Zacconi's excerpt (Ex. 2) is entitled *contrapunto sopra il qui di sotto canto fermo á nota contra nota*.

EXAMPLE 1

Mozart (Fux)

CF

EXAMPLE 2

Lodovico Zacconi: *Prattica de musica* seconda parte, 1622

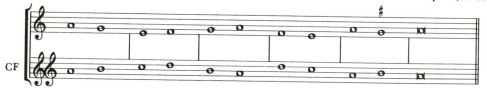

CF

II. Second Species (2:1)

Only consonance and dissonant passing-tone minims are allowed against the *cantus*. See the section dealing with passing tones in chapter 3.

The Mozart excerpt of Ex. 3 is original; the leaps in the counterpointing voice near the cadence are somewhat unusual. Berardi's illustration of this species in Ex. 4 employs only consonant intervals.

EXAMPLE 3

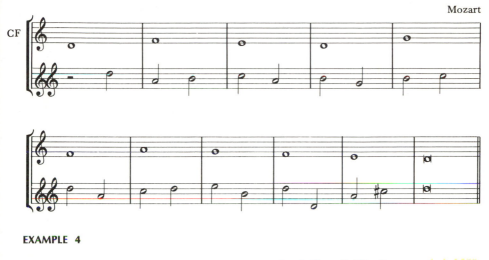

Mozart

EXAMPLE 4

Angelo Berardi: *Miscellanea musicale* 1689

III. Third Species (4:1)

The semiminims in the counterpointing part may incorporate consonant intervals (both stepwise and by leap), as well as passing tones on the off-beat, auxiliaries, *portamentos*, and *cambiata* figures (see chapter 5).

Mozart's Ex. 5 is again original. The selection from Diruta (*contrapunto di note negre*) shown in Ex. 6 employs a few eighth notes as well; note the *portamento* in meas. 6. The same *cantus* is also used for earlier illustrations of first and second species in his treatise. In both excerpts, no instances of accented passing tones (dissonant on the beat) may be found.

EXAMPLE 5

Mozart

(continues on following pg.)

EXAMPLE 5   *(continued)*

EXAMPLE 6

Girolamo Diruta: *Il Transilvano* (book 2) 1609

IV. Fourth Species (2:1 with syncopes)

Syncopes (tied minims) incorporating consonance and suspensions are now permitted. See the section dealing with suspensions in chapter 3.

With the exception of the notated changes, Mozart copies Fux in Ex. 7. Although Morley does not follow a strict species approach, he does employ a technique of discant writing; the same original *cantus* shown in Ex. 8 (note the F♯) is used for most of his two-voice examples. Observe that the upper voice imitates the pitch series of the *cantus* at the octave! The diminished fifth in measure 4 is curious. The passage becomes rhythmically free near the cadence.

EXAMPLE 7

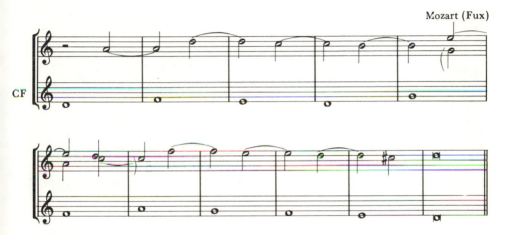

EXAMPLE 8

Thomas Morley: *A Plain and Easy Introduction* (part 2) 1597

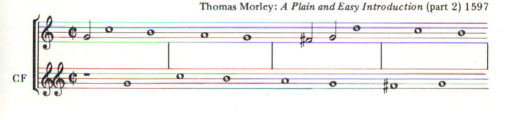

V. Fifth Species ("free":1)

The counterpointing voice is now rhythmically free, with all typical melodic idioms and use of dissonance available.

The fifth-species selection of Ex. 9 is original with Mozart; observe the irregular upper ornamentation of the suspension in measure 4. Zarlino employs only examples of first species (*contrapunto semplice*) and fifth species (*contrapuncto diminutio*) in conjunction with *cantus firmus* technique; see Ex. 10.

The following excerpt illustrated in Ex. 11 from Adriano Banchieri's *Cartella musicale* (1614) is worth reproducing in light of its remarkable resemblance to Fux's later approach.

EXAMPLE 9

EXAMPLE 10

Gioseffo Zarlino: *Le Istitutione harmoniche* (part 3) 1558

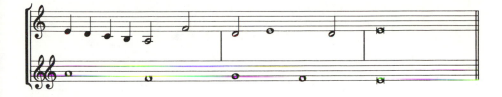

EXAMPLE 11

Adriano Banchieri: *Cartella musicale* 1614

Canto Fermo

Primo Contrapunto

Secundo Contrapunto

Terzo Contrapunto

(continues on following pg.)

EXAMPLE 11   (*continued*)

VI. Three Voices: First Species

The procedure used in two-voice writing is now applied in the same manner to other textures. The one excerpt of Ex. 12 will suffice; only consonance is allowed. Mozart again resorts to Fux; note the octave displacement near the cadence.

EXAMPLE 12

Mozart (Fux)

CF

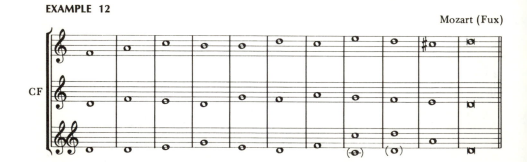

Appendix 2

The Mass

The Mass comprises the most extensive source of sacred polyphony of the sixteenth century. This appendix will discuss briefly the format of the Mass as it pertains to musical settings of the period.

The Mass, as the main liturgical service of the Roman Catholic Church, is centered around the celebration of the Eucharist, the sanctification and distribution of the body and blood of Christ to the congregation. The text is divided into two parts: the *Ordinary*, whose text remains constant through each ceremony, and the *Proper*, whose text changes from Sunday to Sunday according to the Liturgical Year or calendar.

A composer's setting of a Mass is generally understood to consist only of the five movements of the Ordinary: Kyrie, Gloria, Credo, Sanctus, and Agnus Dei. In a Requiem Mass (*Missa pro defunctis*), the Gloria and Credo are omitted, and some substitution in the Proper is made. The titles used for the identification of polyphonic Masses usually refer to preexistent musical sources on which the Mass is based. For example, Palestrina's *Missa Laude Sion* is a parody of his own motet of the same name, which in turn is based on the Gregorian sequence. The Proper of the Mass provided composers with different texts for polyphonic settings. These were usually designated as motets.

The following format illustrates those sections of the Mass normally employed for polyphonic settings:

Ordinary	**Proper**
(*Ordinarium Missae*)	(*Properium Missae*)
	1. Introit
2. Kyrie	
3. Gloria	
	4. Gradual
	5. Alleluia
	(6). Sequence (on some Feast days)
7. Credo	8. Offertory
9. Sanctus	
10. Agnus Dei	11. Communion

The Latin text of the Ordinary is reproduced below along with a brief comment on the polyphonic setting of each movement.

1.   Kyrie Eleison

Kýrie eléison, Chríste eléison, Kýrie eléison

The only part of the Mass in Greek, this movement features intense polyphonic texture as a result of the brevity of the text. It is divided into three parts, each of which constitutes a self-contained section with a strongly articulated cadence: Kyrie, Christe, Kyrie. (The second Kyrie almost always features new musical material). The threefold repetition of each part of the text, typical of chant settings of this movement, is not normally adhered to in contrapuntal settings.

2.   Gloria in Excelsis Deo

(Glória in excélsis Déo.) Et in térra pax homínibus bónae voluntátis, Laudámus te. Benedícimus te. Adorámus te. Glorificámus te. Grátias ágimus tibi própter mágnam glóriam túam. Dómine Déus, Rex caeléstis, Déus Páter omnípotens. Dómine Fíli unigénite Jésu Chríste. Dómine Déus, Agnus Déi, Fílius Pátris. Qui tóllis peccáta múndi, miserére nóbis. Qui tóllis peccáta múndi, súscipe deprecatiónem nóstram. Qui sédes ad déxteram Pátris, miserére nóbis. Quóniam tu sólus sánctus. Tu sólus Dóminus. Tu sólus altíssimus, Jésu Chríste. Cum Sáncto Spíritu, in glória Déi Pátris. Amen.

The opening phrase is intoned by the priest. The length of both the Gloria and following Credo is such that it favors less extensive imitative treatment and more homorhythmic texture. There is generally less "development" or use of reentries. This movement customarily is divided into two sections, with the second beginning at the *Qui Tollis.*

3.   Credo

(Crédo in únum Déum.) Pátrem omnipoténtem, factórem caéli et térrae, visibílium ómnium, et invisibílium. Et in únum Dóminum Jésum Chrístum, Fílium Déi unigénitum. Et ex Pátre nátum ante ómnia saécula. Déum de Déo, lúmen de lúmine, Déum vérum de Déo véro. Génitum, non fáctum, consubstantiálem Pátri: per quem ómnia facta sunt. Qui própter nos hómines, et própter nóstram salútem descéndit de caélis. Et incarnátus est de Spíritu Sáncto ex María Vírgine: Et hómo fáctus est. Crucifíxus étiam pro nóbis: sub Póntio Piláto pássus, et sepúltus est. Et resurréxit tértia díe, secúndum Scriptúras. Et ascéndit in caélum: sédet ad déxteram Pátris. Et itérum ventúrus est cum glória, judicáre vívos et mórtuos: cújus régni non érit fínis. Et in Spíritum Sánctum, Dóminum, et vivificántem: qui ex Pátre, Filióque procédit. Qui cum Pátre, et Fílio simul adorátur, et conglorificátur: qui locútus est per Prophétas. Et únam sánctam cathólicam et apostólicam Ecclésiam. Confíteor únum baptísma in remissiónem peccatórum. Et exspécto resurrectiónem mortuórum. Et vítam ventúri sáeculi. Amen.

The initial phrase *Credo in unum Deum* is intoned by the priest. The above remarks on the Gloria apply here as well. The movement is often sectioned into three distinct parts, with new beginnings at the *Crucifixus* and *Et in Spiritum Sanctum*. One interesting tradition is the setting of the *Et incarnatus est*, which normally employs long note values.

4.   Sanctus

Sánctus, Sánctus, Sánctus, Dóminus Déus Sábaoth. Pléni sunt caéli et térra glória túa. Hosánna in excélsis.—Benedíctus qui vénit in nómine Dómini. Hosánna in excélsis.

This movement is typically divided into four distinct and self-contained sections: Sanctus, Hosanna, Benedictus, and repeat of the Hosanna. The Sanctus and Benedictus feature considerable polyphonic treatment, with the Benedictus usually set for a smaller number of voices. The Hosanna is often cast in a homorhythmic style with frequent use of triple meter.

5.   Agnus Dei

Ágnus Déi, qui tóllis peccáta múndi: miserére nóbis. Ágnus Déi, qui tóllis peccáta múndi: miserére nóbis. Ágnus Déi, qui tóllis peccáta múndi: dóna nóbis pácem.

There are often two distinct settings of this movement, the first employing the *Miserere nobis,* and the final one concluding with the *Dona nobis pacem.* Again, extensive polyphonic procedures prevail.

Major Composers and Theorists

The major composers and theorists of the Late Renaissance are listed below with their attendant dates. Those whose works are illustrated in this text with representative excerpts or complete movements, are denoted with an asterisk; a listing of the various sections may be found in the composer index. For the sake of convenience they are grouped according to nationalistic or stylistic traits, although in a few instances this classification is only approximate.

Flemish

*Josquin des Prez (c. 1445-1521)
*Heinrich Isaac (c. 1450-1517)
*Pierre de la Rue (c. 1460-1518)
*Nicholas Gombert (c. 1490-c. 1560)
 Jacobus Clemens non Papa (c. 1510-1557)
*Phillipe de Monte (1521-1603)
*Roland de Lassus (Lasso) (1532-1594)
*Jan Pieterszoon Sweelinck (1562-1621)

French

*Jean Mouton (c. 1460-1522)
 Clément Janequin (c. 1485-1560)
 Claudin de Sermisy (c. 1490-1562)

Claude Goudimel (c. 1505-1572)
Claude Le Jeune (c. 1528-1600)
*Guillaume Costeley (1531-1606)

Roman

*Giovanni Pierluigi da Palestrina (c. 1525-1594)
Giovanni Maria Nanini (c. 1543-1607)
*Marc Antonio Ingegneri (c. 1545-1592)

Italian

Phillipe Verdelot (c. 1490-c. 1545)
Constanza Festa (c. 1495-1545)
Jacques Arcadelt (c. 1504-c. 1567)
Orazi Vecchi (1550-1605)
Luca Marenzio (1553-1599)
*Carlo Gesualdo (1560-1613)
*Claudio Monteverdi (1567-1643)

Venetian

Adrian Willaert (c. 1485-1562)
*Cipriano de Rore (1516-1565)
*Andrea Gabrieli (c. 1510-1586)
*Giovanni Gabrieli (1557-1612)

Spanish

*Cristóbal Morales (c. 1500-1553)
Luis Milán (c. 1500-1561)
Antonio de Cabezón (1510-1566)
*Tomás Luis de Victoria (1548-1611)

German

Heinrich Finck (c. 1445-1527)
Ludwig Senfl (1492-1555)
Jakob Handl (Gallus) (1550-1591)
*Hans Leo Hassler (1564-1612)

English

John Taverner (1494-1545)
*Christopher Tye (c. 1500-1573)
Thomas Tallis (c. 1505-1585)
*William Byrd (1543-1623)
*Thomas Morley (1557-1603)

*Thomas Tompkins (1571-1656)
*John Wilbye (1574-1638)
*Thomas Weelkes (1575-1623)
*Orlando Gibbons (1583-1625)

Theorists*

Johannes Tinctoris (c. 1435-1511)
Franchino Gafori (Gafurius) (1451-1522)
Pietro Aaron (Aron) (1480-1545)
Henricus Glareanus (1488-1563)
*Nicola Vicentino (1511-1572)
Francisco de Salinas (1513-1590)
*Gioseffo Zarlino (1517-1590)
*Vincenzo Galilei (1520-1591)
*Ludovico Zacconi (1555-1627)
*Thomas Morley (1557-1603)
*Girolamo Diruta (1557-1612)
*Adriano Banchieri (1568-1634)
*Angelo Berardi (1653-1700)
Johann Fux (1660-1741)

*(Although the last two theorists belong properly in the seventeenth and eighteenth centuries respectively, their writings did focus on Late Renaissance techniques).

Bibliography

The following entries constitute a selected bibliography and, as such, are not intended to be comprehensive. Annotations are included for all except the final two categories. Only English sources and translations are listed.

I. TEXTS

Only texts dealing with the study of polyphony as related to the stylistic practice of the Late Renaissance are listed. Such books as Salzer and Schachter *Counterpoint in Composition* (New York: McGraw-Hill, 1969), which incorporates a species counterpoint approach as an introduction to the linear analysis of tonal music, have been omitted. The manuals have been divided into two classifications: those employing species as opposed to those utilizing a more "direct" method.

Species

Fux, Johann Joseph,   *The Study of Counterpoint.* Translated and edited from *Gradus ad Parnassum* 1725 by Alfred Mann. New York: W. W. Norton & Company, Inc., 1965. 156 pages.

Mann, Alfred,   *The Study of Fugue* (pages 75-138 contain a portion of Fux's *Gradus* not translated in the above entry). New York: W. W. Norton & Company, Inc., 1965. 339 pages.

The two above listings represent the extent of material from Fux's treatise currently available in English translation from the original Latin. Reference to this most crucial manual has already been made in appendix 1. Mann draws his two excerpts from the second volume of Fux's text, entitled *Pars Activa,* which in turn is divided into two basic sections, the first dealing with use of a *cantus firmus,* and the second devoted to study of fugue and double counterpoint (these correspond to the two entries above).

This treatise is cast in the form of a dialogue between master and pupil. Fux never states that he intends to base his study of contrapuntal practice on the practice of the Late Renaissance; he does, however, identify the master Aloysius with Palestrina, himself. Although Fux's rules coincide remarkably well with sixteenth-century style, there are, nevertheless, occasional discrepancies; in particular, his handling of rhythm often relates more to eighteenth-century practice (this is particularly true in some of the fugal writing). Even chromatic voice-leading occurs in the later passages, suggesting a more baroque flavor.

The importance of Fux's contribution, however, lies in his systematic introduction to the study of counterpoint through the species. This pedagogical method was not only retained in subsequent manuals of Renaissance polyphony (see Jeppesen below), but also profoundly influenced all teaching of counterpoint, even in tonal idioms (both Schenker's and Schönberg's approach are rooted in species).

Jeppesen, Knud,   *Counterpoint: The Polyphonic Vocal Style of the Sixteenth Century.* Translated by Glen Haydon. Englewood Cliffs: Prentice-Hall, Inc. 1939. 302 pages.

The classic exposition of Fux's species approach in the present century, Jeppesen carries species through four-voice texture, while also introducing imitative procedures and combinations of various species. There is great attention given to the discussion of those idioms stylistic to the period, much of which resulted from the research in his earlier *Palestrina and the Dissonance* (the English translation appeared in 1927). Although it seems slightly out of place in a practical text of this nature, the introductory chapter outlining the history of contrapuntal theory is excellent, mentioning some thirty-odd theorists ranging from Hucbald to Riemann. The opening section of technical features includes observations on Renaissance melody and harmonic resources. Later chapters deal with writing for more than four voices, canon, motet, Mass, and the "vocal fugue." There is little discussion of the relationship of microrhythm as related to text setting, and few examples from literature in two- and three-voice texture. The text uses the C clefs throughout.

Swindale, Owen,   *Polyphonic Composition*. London: Oxford University Press, 1962.
    140 pages.

This is an interesting though somewhat neglected text. After a brief introduction to plainsong, the author commences with a species approach in two-voice texture; his employment of real chants as *cantus firmi* and the use of text (even in first species) is worthy of comment. Following a belated discussion of the sixteenth-century "modal system," there is an extensive section devoted to two-part "fugal style." The rest of the manual is taken up with presentations of homorhythmic texture, "fantasia on a plainsong," fugal style, and motet, all in three voices. There is some material on triple meter, double counterpoint, and four-part writing. His handling of compositional devices is generally quite comprehensive, although he has some quaint ideas about two-voice suspensions (see pp. 30-32), and the $^6_5$ is only slightly mentioned (p. 85). The text contains a number of examples from literature, but few extensive works are quoted. The index is useful.

Non-Species or Direct

Basset, Leslie,   *Manual of Sixteenth Century Counterpoint*. New York: Appleton-Century-Crofts, 1967. 55 pages.

This small manual appears to be a condensation of Soderlund (see below). After a discussion of two- and three-voice texture, only two pages are devoted to "multi-voiced writing." The list of devices (consonant 4th, double suspension, augmented triads, etc.) at the end of the book is useful. All examples are taken from actual literature, and are cross-referenced to the older Soderlund anthology (see below).

Benjamin, Thomas,   *The Craft of Modal Counterpoint: A Practical Approach*. New York: Schirmer Books, 1979. 230 pages.

One of the more useful aspects of this manual is that it serves as both a text and anthology at the same time; some nineteen complete movements are quoted (fifteen of which appear in an appendix and range from two- to five-voice texture). This is in addition to numerous other lengthy excerpts from literature. Like Soderlund, (see below), the author takes a "direct" approach to the contrapuntal practice of the period. After an introductory chapter which lays the foundation for rhythmic, harmonic, and melodic practices in general, the following chapters deal with two- through four-voice contrapuntal settings, with a final section devoted to the motet. Many of the assignments are quite ingenious. They contain problems in which only an incomplete texture is included in a composition taken from the literature, and the student is asked to fill in the remaining parts.

Merrit, Arthur T., *Sixteenth Century Polyphony*. Cambridge: Harvard University Press, 1939. 215 pages.

A curious book with some revealing insights into the style of the period. The opening lengthy section (28 pages) is devoted to plainsong. The succeeding "Analysis of Contrapuntal Technique" is just that—an extensive analytical discussion of polyphonic idioms dealing with such questions as rhythm, single-line melodies and lines in combination, harmony, etc. Although this section might prove confusing to a beginner, it would be, on the other hand, quite useful as a review for advanced students. The "Application of Contrapuntal Technique" that follows is basically a practical exposition of two- to four-voice writing in a nonspecies approach. There is a good treatment of microrhythm, although the $\frac{6}{5}$ is never clearly isolated or identified. The text includes some six excerpts or complete pieces from literature, some of which are extensively analyzed. The list of scholarly collections of contrapuntal music (mostly complete works and sets such as Denkmäler) is excellent, although somewhat dated.

Morris, R. O., *Contrapuntal Technique in the Sixteenth Century*. London: Oxford University Press, 1922. 74 pages plus examples.

This treatise can hardly be considered a practical text, since no didactic approach or student assignments are employed. It consists basically of a series of chapters devoted to general comments on the stylistic practice of the period: "Modal system," "Rhythm," "Melody," "Harmony," "Design," etc. The opening "Point of View" severely criticizes the *cantus firmus* and species method of teaching counterpoint, and advocates in its place a freer or more "direct" manner of dealing with the music. Although some of the discussion is quite informative (for example, the sections on rhythm and melody), other areas are radically abbreviated in their treatment (the consideration of dissonance in *all* textures is included in a short twelve-page chapter on harmony). The examples of music are collected together at the conclusion of the book; although they are almost all from literature, most are very short, with few complete pieces given, and the incorporation of text is inconsistent. (The few original examples carry the pseudonym "Bugsworthy, *Conceits and Vapours* No. 10001"). The final section of text is devoted to technical aspects of the English school, for which Morris seems to show some degree of prejudice.

Krenek, Ernst, *Modal Counterpoint in the Style of the Sixteenth Century*. London: Boosey and Hawkes, Inc., 1959. 21 pages.

This briefest of outlines includes "Vocabulary," "Melodic Characteristics" (note that text setting is included under "Motet"), and "Two- and Three-Part Writing" only. No examples are given of such devices as counterpoint at the twelfth, etc., while the term *suspension* is avoided altogether! There is a short appendix on species approach using a Fux *cantus*. All the examples of music are original.

Soderlund, Gustave Fredric,   *Direct Approach to Counterpoint in Sixteenth-Century Style*. Englewood Cliffs, NJ: Prentice-Hall, Inc., 1947. 133 pages.

As the title implies, this important text bypasses the traditional species method in favor of a more "direct" introduction to the stylistic practice of the period. After a preliminary section dealing with the individual melodic line, the author proceeds through the contrapuntal combination of two, three, and four and more voices, beginning in each case with white-note values, and then adding black durations with their various idiomatic settings. Except for some note-against-note writing in semibreves, the species approach is avoided throughout. Meticulous attention is given to specific stylistic devices (such as the $\frac{6}{3}$) with numerous short examples supplied. Indeed, the number of illustrations becomes almost overwhelming at times, with about eighty (!) excerpts from literature cited in discussing skips in the single melodic line. This manual has the great advantage of being written in conjunction with the author's anthology of sacred music from this period (see below), so that countless references are made to the accompanying volume; this doubtless accounts for the fact that only one complete work from literature is included in the text proper. In addition to the emphasis given to text setting and rhythm as they relate to the individual vocal line (microrhythm), there are sections devoted to Latin pronunciation, homophonic writing, and polychoral procedures.

II. HISTORICAL TREATISES (AVAILABLE IN ENGLISH)

Fifteenth Century

Gafurius, Franchinus,   *Practica Musicae*. Translated and transcribed by Clement A. Miller. Rome: American Institute of Musicology, 1968.
Tinctoris, Johannes,   *Liber de arte contrapuncti*. Translated and edited by Albert Seay. Rome: American Institute of Musicology, 1961.

The Gafurius and Tinctoris treatises relate properly to the polyphonic practice of the fifteenth-century, being dated 1496 and 1477 respectively. Nevertheless, their formulation of certain contrapuntal concepts had a great influence on the theoretical writing of the following hundred years. In general, they avoid the more didactic approach of many of the later treatises and tend to comment on the basic voice-leading principles of their period, compiling a list of tendencies (or "rules") which personify the prevalent style. The sets of eight rules proposed by each author overlap in many instances; they are illustrated by original examples or, in the case of Tinctoris, by various excerpts taken from actual literature.

Sixteenth Century

Morley, Thomas,   *A Plain and Easy Introduction to Practical Music*. 2nd ed. Edited by R. Alec Harman. New York: W. W. Norton & Company, Inc., 1963.

The second and third parts of this important document (dated 1597) are entitled, "Treating of Descant" and "Treating of Composing or Setting Songs." The descant section is organized in a loosely structured species approach, beginning with two-voice writing (see appendix 1 for the *cantus* which Morley uses throughout this part). His study of three-voice texture is based on a different *cantus*, with some degree of freedom permitted. The final section involves "free" contrapuntal settings in three to six voices. His comments on canonic technique are particularly interesting and extensive. The format of the treatise is the typical dialogue between master and student, which is echoed later in Fux's manual. One should be forewarned that many of the idioms are those associated with the English school near the end of the century and occasionally conflict with the more conservative practices on the continent.

Zarlino, Gioseffo,   *Le Istitutioni harmoniche* (Part III). Translated by Guy A. Marco and Claude V. Palisca. New York: W. W. Norton & Company, Inc., 1976.

Doubtless the most comprehensive and carefully organized compendium on counterpoint during the period, this treatise of 1558 includes a discussion of consonance and dissonance, voice-leading between consonances, two-voice writing based on a *cantus* (beginning with note-against-note or *semplice* and progressing immediately to free or *diminuto*), canon (*fuga*) vs. imitation, cadences, double counterpoint, three- and four-voice writing, and various rhythmic problems. Although Zarlino cites composers in his text, all of the musical examples are original. The English edition is excellent, with important terminology given in the original Italian.

III. ANTHOLOGIES

The five anthologies listed below devote all or a significant amount of their content to compositions of the sixteenth century. No attempt has been made to include either editions of complete works of specific composers of the period or scholarly collections (such as the Denkmäler or Chorwerk series).

Brandt, William, et al.   *The Comprehensive Study of Music: Anthology of Music from Plainchant through Gabrieli.* Vol. I. New York: Harper & Row, Pub., 1980. 318 pages.

The last 194 pages of this collection are devoted to sacred and secular music of the sixteenth century. Only translations are provided; the clear layout of the scores is occasionally marred by an incorrect note. Reference has been made earlier to the six settings of the *O magnum mysterium* text, which serve as the basis for a useful comparison of various composers.

Davidson, Archibald T., and Apel, Willi,   *Historical Anthology of Music.* Vol. I (revised edition). Cambridge: Harvard University Press, 1950. 258 pages.

This classic anthology devotes its final 120 pages to vocal and instrumental music from the early sixteenth century to Sweelinck. Translations, an index, and historical comments are included. The works have been transcribed in modern rhythmic notation, with the ♩ usually = ♩. The vocal pieces are often in condensed score, with the result that, in some instances, the texts of the individual voices are difficult to follow.

Hardy, Gordon, and Fish, Arnold,   *Music Literature: A Workbook for Analysis.* Vol. II (Polyphony). New York: Dodd, Mead, and Co., 1967. 328 pages.

Pages 182 to 251 contain complete movements of polyphony from the sixteenth century, ranging from Josquin to Morley. No analytical comment is provided, although translations of the texts are included. The textures range from two to five voices. In some cases the scholarly sources for the reprints are given.

Palisca, Claude V.,   *Norton Anthology of Western Music.* Vol. I. New York: W. W. Norton & Company, Inc., 1980. 644 pages.

Although the first volume of this series includes selections from the medieval through the baroque periods, pages 94 to 293 contain an excellent assortment of works from the Renaissance, arranged in order of genre. Because the pieces are drawn from different scholarly editions with sources cited, the format of the notation tends to vary from one composition to the other. Translations are included.

Soderlund, Gustave Fredric, and Scott, Samuel H.,   *Examples of Gregorian Chant and Sacred Music of the Sixteenth Century.* Englewood Cliffs: Prentice-Hall, Inc., 1971. 303 pages.

This valuable anthology is a revision by Scott of the earlier edition of Soderlund, first published by Appleton-Century-Crofts, which was intended as a supplemental volume of examples to his counterpoint text (see above). The collection is divided into three sections: Gregorian chant, examples of movements from two- through five-voice texture, and four masses by Palestrina, either given complete or in excerpts. Scott has greatly expanded the number of two- and three-voice compositions, while omitting certain useful examples (including the Responses of Ingeneri and all instances of polychoral writing). Soderlund's original commentaries and translations, which were already sadly deficient, have not been revised despite the large number of new works inserted. The value of this anthology is thus diminished by the lack of a truly systematic guide to the structures, idioms, and devices to be found in the various compositions. Treble and bass clefs are employed, but some of the new pieces are given in modern notation with a semiminim beat, thus creating a confusing situation for the student at times (this despite Scott's reason to the contrary in the Foreword).

IV. RELATED BOOKS, ARTICLES, AND ANALYSES

The list of sources below will serve as supplemental reading in the subject of polyphonic practice in the Late Renaissance.

Books*

Andrews, H. K.   *The Technique of Byrd's Vocal Polyphony*. New York: Oxford University Press, 1966.

Andrews, H. K.   *An Introduction to the Technique of Palestrina*. London: Novello and Co., 1958.

Apel, Willi.   *The Notation of Polyphonic Music 900-1600*. 4th edition. Cambridge: Medieval Academy of America, 1953.

Barbour, J. Murray.   *Tuning and Temperament: A Historical Study*. New York: Da Capo Press, 1972.

Brown, Howard M.   *Embellishing Sixteenth-Century Music*. London: Oxford University Press, 1976.

Brown, Howard M.   *Music in the Renaissance*. London: Oxford University Press, 1976.

Donington, Robert.   *The Interpretation of Early Music*. London: Faber & Faber, 1974.

Einstein, Alfred.   *The Italian Madrigal*. (in three volumes) Translated by Krappe, Sessions, and Strunk. Princeton: Princeton University Press, 1949.

Fellowes, Edmund.   *The English Madrigal Composers*. London: Oxford University Press, 1921.

Jeppesen, Knud.   *The Style of Palestrina and the Dissonance*. Translated by Margaret Hamerik (reprinted by Dover, 1970).

*(No dissertations are included in this list)

Lowinsky, Edward.   *The Secret Chromatic Art in the Netherlands Motet*. trans. by Carl Buchman. New York: Columbia University Press, 1946.

Lowinsky, Edward.   *Tonality and Atonality in Sixteenth-Century Music*. Berkeley: University of California Press, 1961.

Mendel, Arthur.   *Pitch in Western Music since 1500: A Re-examination*. Basel: Bärenreiter Kassel, 1979.

Reese, Gustave.   *Music in the Renaissance*. New York: W. W. Norton & Company, Inc., 1954.

Rubio, Samuel P.   *Classical Polyphony*. Translated by Thomas Rive. Oxford: Basil Blackwell, 1972.

Sparks, Edgar H.   *Cantus Firmus in Mass and Motet 1420-1520*. Berkeley: University of California Press, 1963.

Strunk, Oliver.   *Source Readings in Music History*. New York: W. W. Norton & Company, Inc., 1950.

Those works of Andrews (*Palestrina*), Fellowes, Jeppesen, and Rubio are particularly relevant as regards the material in this text.

Articles

Aldrich, Putnam.   "An Approach to the Analysis of Renaissance Music." *Music Review*, 30/1 (1969), pp. 1–21.

Bashour, Frederick.   "Toward a More Rigorous Methodology in the Analysis of the Pre-Tonal Repertory." *College Music Symposium*, 19/2 (Fall 1979), pp. 140–153.

Bergquist, Peter.   "Mode and Polyphony around 1500." *The Music Forum*, vol. I, pp. 99–161.

Cohen, Dalia.   "Palestrina Counterpoint: A Music Expression of Unexcited Speech." *Journal of Music Theory*, 15/1 & 2 (1971), pp. 84–111.

Fox, Charles Warren.   "Non-Quartal Harmony in the Renaissance." *Musical Quarterly*, 31/1 (1945), pp. 33–53.

Godt, Irving.   "Renaissance Paraphrase Technique: A Descriptive Tool." *Music Theory Spectrum*, 2 (1980), pp. 110–18.

Haar, James.   "False Relations and Chromaticism in Sixteenth-Century Music." *Journal of the American Musicological Society*, 30/3 (Fall 1977), pp. 391–418.

Haigh, Andrew.   "Modal Harmony in the Music of Palestrina." *Essays in Honor of Archibald T. Davidson*. Cambridge: Harvard University Press, 1957, pp. 111–120.

Hanson, John.   "Enumeration of Dissonance in the Masses of Palestrina." *College Music Symposium*, 23/1 (1983), pp. 50–64.

Hanson, John.   "Pedagogy of Sixteenth-Century Counterpoint: Selected Examples with Commentary." *Theory and Practice*, 4/1 (March 1979), pp. 5–14.

Harran, Don.   "New Evidence for Musica Ficta: The Cautionary Sign." *Journal of the American Musicological Society*, 29/1 (Spring 1976), pp. 77–98.

Isgro, Robert.   "Sixteenth-Century Conception of Harmony." *College Music Symposium*, 19/1 (Spring 1979), pp. 7–53.

Leichtentritt, Hugo,   "The Reform of Trent and its Effect on Music." *Musical Quarterly*, 30/3 (1944), pp. 319–28.

Lenaerts, R. G.   "The Sixteenth-Century Parody Mass in the Netherlands." *Musical Quarterly*, 36/3 (1950), pp. 410–21.

Lewin, David.   "An Interesting Global Rule for Species Counterpoint." *In Theory Only* 6/8 (1983), pp. 19–44.

Lockwood, Lewis.   "On 'Parody' as Term and Concept in Sixteenth-Century Music." *Aspects of Medieval and Renaissance Music*, ed. by Jan La Rue. New York: W. W. Norton & Company, Inc., 1966, pp. 560–75.

Loach, Donald.   "A Stylistic Approach to Species Counterpoint." *Journal of Music Theory*, 1/2 (November 1957), pp. 181–200.

Lowinsky, Edward.   "Early Scores in Manuscript." *Journal of the American Musicological Society*, 13/1-3 (1960), pp. 126–73.

Marshall, R. L.   "The Paraphrase Technique of Palestrina in His Masses Based on Hymns." *Journal of the American Musicological Society*, 16/3 (1963), pp. 347–72.

Miller, Clement A.   "The Dodecachordon: Its Origins and Influence on Renaissance Musical Thought." *Musica Disciplina* 15 (1961), pp. 156–66.

Palisca, Claude V.   "Vincenzo Galilei's Counterpoint Treatise: A Code for the Seconda Pratica." *Journal of the American Musicological Society*, 9/2 (Summer 1956), pp. 81–96.

Quereau, Quentin W.   "Aspects of Palestrina's Parody Procedure." *Journal of Musicology* 1 (1982), pp. 198–216.

Quereau, Quentin W.   "Sixteenth-Century Parody: An Approach to Analysis." *Journal of the American Musicological Society*, 31/3 (Fall 1978), pp. 407–41.

Rivera, Benito.   "Harmonic Theory in Musical Treatises of the Late Fifteenth and Early Sixteenth-Centuries." *Music Theory Spectrum*, 1 (1979), pp. 80–95.

Rivera, Benito.   "The Isagoge (1581) of Johannes Avianius: An Early Formulation of Triadic Theory." *Journal of Music Theory*, 22/1 (Spring 1978), pp. 43–64.

Stern, David.   "Tonal Organization in Modal Polyphony." *Theory and Practice*, 6/2 (1981), pp. 5–11.

Wienpahl, Robert W.   "Zarlino, the Senerio and Tonality." *Journal of the American Musicological Society*, 12/1 (Spring 1959), pp. 27–41.

Analyses

Cogan, Robert, and Escot, Pozzi.   *Sonic Design: The Nature of Sound and Music.* Englewood Cliffs: Prentice-Hall, Inc., 1976.
Lassus: *Bon Jour, Mon Coeur* (pages 130–41).

Godt, Irving.   "A New Look at Palestrina's *Missa Papae Marcelli*." *College Music Symposium*, 23/1 (1983), pp. 22–49.

Jeppesen, Knud.   "Problems of the Pope Marcellus Mass." tr. by Lewis Lockwood. *Norton Critical Scores: Palestrina's Pope Marcellus Mass.* Ed. by Lewis Lockwood, pp. 99–130.

Mitchell, William.   "The Prologue to Orlando de Lasso's *Prophetiae Sibyllarum*." *The Music Forum*, 2 (1970), pp. 264–73.

Novak, Saul.   "Fusion of Design and Tonal Order in Mass and Motet: Josquin Desprez and Heinrich Isaac." *Music Forum*, 2 (1970).
Josquin: *Missa Pange lingua* (pp. 206–31).
Isaac: *Missa Carminum* and *Innsbruck, ich muss dich lassen* (p. 231–63).

Salzer, Felix.   "Heinrich Schenker and Historical Research: Monteverdi's Madrigal *Oimè, se tanto amate*." *Aspects of Schenkerian Theory* Ed. by David Beach. New Haven: Yale University Press, 1983, pp. 135–52.

Salzer, Felix.   *Structural Hearing: Tonal Coherence in Music.* Two volumes. (reprinted by Dover 1962).
Vol. II includes linear analyses of excerpts from:
 Gesualdo: *Io pur respiro* (pp. 256–57).
 Lassus: *Recordare Jesu pie* (pp. 166–67).
 Marenzio: *Io piango* (pp. 264–67).
Salzer, Felix, and Schachter, Carl.   *Counterpoint in Composition.* New York: McGraw-Hill Book Company, 1969.
 Palestrina: Agnus Dei I (*Missa Veni Sponsa Christi*) (pp. 413–18).
 Victoria: *O Vos Omnes* (pp. 419–24).
Schmidt, Kenneth.   "Harmonic Progressions in the Music of Gesualdo: An analysis of *O Vos Omnes.*" *In Theory Only,* 1/3, pp. 6–16.

Index of Names
and Works

References to composers or authors in the text are indexed below. References to specific works are listed below their respective author. Short examples or excerpts are denoted in roman type (Ex. 3-2), while longer sections or complete movements are indicated with bold type (**Ex. 4-1**).

Index of Terms

A *cappella* singing, 4
Accidentals (*see* Musica ficta)
Agogic accent, 22–23
Alla breve, 187, 188, 192
Altus, 1
Antiphonal writing, 67, 234, 243, 244
Augmented sixth chord, 258
Augmented triad, 257
Authentic modes, 6–8
Auxiliary (neighboring) tone:
  in melodic lines, 37
  in two-voice texture, 43, 281
  producing parallel dissonance, 96–97

Bar lines, 5–6
Basso sequente, 27
Bassus, 1
Battuta, 4
Beat, 5, 93, 187, 188, 190
Bicinium, 26
Bi-focal tonality, 143
Black notes:
  in melodic lines, 36–39
  in two-voice texture, 42–47
  in three-voice texture 96–97
  in four-voice texture, 139
  in text setting, 39–41
  in triple meter, 188
Breve, 4–5

Cadence:
  authentic, 88–89, 93, 137, 179–80, 241, 242
  Burgundian, 87–88, 90
  deceptive, 90
  frequency of interior cadential tones in modes, 13

  in canonic technique, 116–17, 131
  in interior phrases, 56–57, 90–91, 184
  in melodic lines, 19–20, 24
  in two-voice texture, 28, 32, 56–57
  in three-voice texture, 87–92
  in four-voice texture, 137–38
  in five- and six-voice texture, 179–80
  in eight-voice texture, 241, 242
  interrupted, 56–57, 58, 91, 116–17, 184
  irregular, 56–57, 264–65
  leading tone, 87–88, 138, 179–80
  overlapping (dovetailing), 91, 107, 122, 128, 147, 184, 198, 236, 239, 251
  Phrygian, 19, 32, 87–88, 112, 138, 179–80, 242
  plagal, 90, 138, 179–80, 241, 242
  with cambiata, 137, 179–80
  with consonant fourth, 93–94, 179–80, 256–57
  with escape tone and passing seventh, 256–57
Cadenza diminuta, 24
Cadenza imperfetta, 137
Cadenza perfetta, 28
Cadenza sfuggita, 56–57
Cadenza semplice, 24
Cambiata (*nota cambiata*):
  filled-in, 38, 43
  in cadences, 137, 179–80
  in combination with passing tones, 96–97
  in melodic lines, 37–38, 120
  in two-voice texture, 44, 281
  older form of, 37–38
Canon:
  asymmetrical point of imitation, 114–16, 133
  cadences in, 116–117, 131
  Cancrizans (crab or retrograde), 53–54, 134, 254–55

307